Needle Felting – To the Point

Needle Felting Techniques

By

Harlan

Farley

This book is dedicated to Margaret
A wonderful patron and a precious friend!
THANK YOU!

Arthur and the Donut in the Stone

Special thanks to Vicky for her invaluable assistance!

FOREWORD:

This is not a book about a specific project or number of similar projects. This is a book about needle felting techniques, whatever your project might be. Most of the included information is geared towards sculptural needle felting but some of the techniques are applicable to flat felting as well.

So what is needle felting? Needle felting is an art/craft using special barbed needles to encourage fiber to felt together. The needles used for needle felting were and are used in the commercial manufacture of various fabrics. Back in the 80s a couple of ingenious people got the idea of using the needles on an individual basis and needle felting was born!

Now it is a growing art/craft form and you'll see needle felted items from tapestries to amazing sculptures. As a medium, needle felting is extremely versatile and has the advantage of being rewarding, whether you are just starting out making your very first project, or you've been doing it for years and your pieces are complex and labor intensive.

So you're interested in needle felting? Well, lets get one thing straight right from the very beginning:

You are going to **BLEED**!!

It is unavoidable when working with extremely sharp needles. The good news is it doesn't hurt all that much and the pokes heal quickly. Also as you become more skilled and practiced at needle felting you become increasingly less likely to jab yourself.

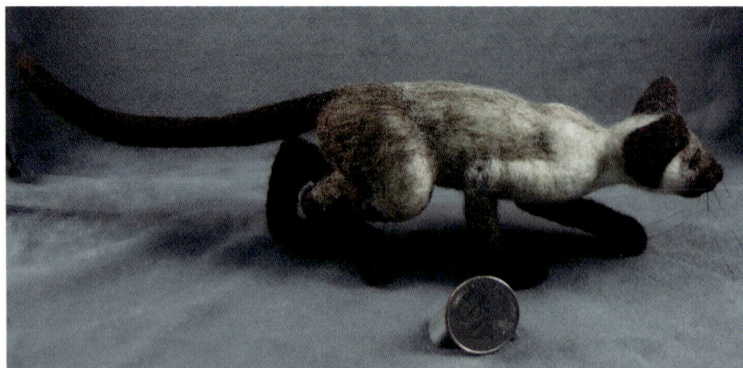

Celery Stalks

There are two main materials used for needle felting: the needles and the fiber. There are also a number of other tools that make needle felting easier but let's start with the basics.

NEEDLES:

Needle felting needles are usually "L" shaped and 3" or 3.5" long.

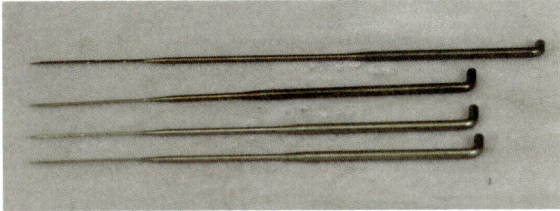

From top to bottom these needles are:
#36
#38 Star
#40
#42

Most needles have triangular shaped tips but there are also needles know as "star" that have four sided tips and even a cone shaped needle that tapers from a very fine tip to a coarser shank. Needles come in a variety of sizes from #36 (largest/coarsest) to #42 (finest). All needle felting needles have barbs but how many barbs a needle may have and where those barbs are located can differ.

Above is the tip of a #36 needle. I've placed a close up of the barbs over the picture of the tip. Depending on where you get your needles, you might purchase a #36 needle that looks identical to this one, or you might purchase one where the barbs are positioned closer to the tip than seen here.

In general, you don't need to be too concerned about the number and placement of the barbs. Most needles sold for needle felting are good and useful tools, but there are differences.

You may see needles described as:

"40 gauge / 2x2x2 barbs / 3 inch" which tells you it is a #40 needle with 2 barbs on each side of the triangular tip.

"36 gauge /6x0x0 barbs / 3.5" is a #36 needle that has 6 barbs that are only one side of the tip.

Most needles I see for sale are described only by their gauge/size. You may find that the #36 needles you buy from one place are completely different in number and location of barbs than needles you buy from another vendor. When you find needles that you really like, remember who sold them to you so you can get more and not be surprised by an unexpected change in the number and placement of barbs.

Storing your needles:

I have plastic collectable card boxes to store my loose needles. I have a separate box for each size of needle and the box is clearly labeled. Store them in a manner to prevent damage to the needles and to yourself.

Color coding your needles:

I recommend color coding your needles by dipping the "L" ends into ink or using a paint pen or some means to identify the size of the needle. I have a small chart taped to my task light that reminds me which color I assigned to which size needle. This practice is very useful!!

You can color code your needles in any number of ways such as dipping them in ink or using a paint pen to color the "L" shaped end.

Just remember to write yourself a chart that explains what the color coding means.

Needles do get dull over time. It generally takes a very long time for a needle to be rendered less useful, but it does happen. This is not something you can see by looking at your needles but this is something you will observe during use. If a needle seems to not work as well as before, it has probably become dull and should be replaced. If you are like me you will feel a great reluctance to just throw it out, but resist the urge to hoard dull needles!! Tape the sharp ends with duct tape prior to throwing them out, but do throw them out!

Needles will also break. Should the tip break off within your fiber/object – remove it! Remove it even if that means taking an Exacto knife to your felted object and cutting it open! Such a cut can be mended but it is important not to leave a tip inside an object. Use duct tape to secure the broken end to the shank before throwing them out. This is a simple safety measure.

FIBER:

Any fiber from a mammal can be felted. Other fibers, such as silk, can also be felted with a different appearance and texture than animal fibers. There is a great variety of texture, appearance and feel just with animal fibers.

Wool is the most commonly used fiber for needle felting. The wide variety of wool is really staggering, but the short of it is different wools vary from extremely coarse to extremely fine in texture. Coarser fiber is easier to felt but will always retain its coarse nature. Fine fiber is more difficult to felt, but can result in a very smooth finished project.

So what fiber should you choose?? Use the fiber you like to work with best. You'll have to find sources for different fibers and try them. Join a needle felting group and exchange fibers with other members, visit a fiber festival in your area, or buy samplers of fibers.

If you want a fiber that is pretty easy to felt and you're not concerned about having a really smooth finished surface you might try Corriedale. If you want a very smooth finished surface you might try Merino. If you want a curly finish you might try Romney.

The fiber on the top is Merino and the fiber below is Corriedale. If you examine the photo carefully you can see that Corriedale is a coarser fiber resulting in a coarser finish than the Merino.

This does not make Merino superior to Corriedale, just different.

The fiber you choose should depend on what fiber you most like using and the finish that you desire for your project.

Most of the fiber you will buy comes "drummed" i.e. it has been processed to align the fibers to run parallel to one another.

Believe me, there are so many types of fiber available and each has its own characteristics AND if that weren't enough there are also "vintages".

Good grief! What does that mean, and do I really need to be concerned?

No! You don't need to be concerned. If you buy Merino this year it will work up pretty much the same way that Merino purchased three years ago did, but to the experienced hand and eye it is possible to see and feel differences between this year's Merino and that of another year. You really don't need to understand that a warm winter or a change in diet can affect the sort of coat a sheep grows. It's just interesting! Well, I think it is interesting!

CORE FIBER:

Whatever your project may be, one of the first decisions you will have to make is whether or not the core will be the same fiber as the surface. It can economically make sense to use a cheaper fiber for the middle or core of your piece, and dress the top with the fiber that you want as your finished surface. Often fiber that is used for a core will felt up faster than a fine finishing fiber, so using a core can save you time as well. However, it can also cause some problems most notably if you have core fiber that you will completely needle through (i.e. from one side of the object clear out the other side). Some of the core fiber will be revealed on the other side. This can be avoided or solved either by carefully surface needling your "dressing fiber" over the core or by redressing areas in which core fiber has been revealed.

Core fiber is not necessarily coarse. Its most notable characteristic is that it has not been drummed to align the fibers. Fibers that are drummed or aligned all run pretty much parallel to one another. Fibers that are mixed up and lay in all directions will felt up faster and more easily than fiber that is aligned.

I use wool batting as my core fiber (see photo).

This batting is sold by the Frankenmuth Woolen Mills and is sold by bed size. I usually purchase batting for a crib and find that quantity lasts a very long time.

Note that the fibers are actually rather fine but they are not aligned significantly which makes this fiber easy to felt and ideal for use as a core fiber.

Storing your fiber:

There are so many options for fiber storage, so what you choose to use should be whatever makes most sense for you. Fiber that is not going to be in use for an extended period of time should be kept in some sort of sealed container to protect it from moths, playful pets or other possible hazards. You can use just about any sealable container whether that is a plastic bag, a plastic box or even a vintage mason jar.

A plastic box with compartments can be useful when you need a variety of smaller quantities of many different colored fibers. I also find the compartments useful for storing custom blends of colors.

The new vacuum bags for food come in sizes that are very suited for the storage of fiber. The elimination of the air will compress the fibers without felting them and save a great deal of storage space. I have personally found these vacuum bags rather unreliable and that over time air does creep in and re-expand the bag.

Fibers of different color that are laid next to one another will, to some degree, exchange fibers. I will often lay a good hank of one color next to a hank of another color and for the most part there is no problem, although occasionally I will find myself picking out the few transferred fibers because their color is significantly different.

ADDITIONAL TOOLS:

WORK SURFACE:

Most needle felters start out working on a dense foam pad or perhaps an old terry cloth towel rolled up. Many, if not the majority, of needle felters continue to work on their dense foam pads or terry cloth towels. Don't!

There is an alternative which is superior and that is the Clover Brush Mat. Buy the large! Even the large brush mat is not extremely large being 6.25" x 4.5" x 2.25". It is a perfect size for small sculpture or flat work and probably would work for larger pieces depending on how you work.

Why?

Foam gives (unless it is solid foam), and over time the needling will cause any foam to break down and need to be replaced. If the foam gives at all, it makes the work harder and is more likely to cause repetitive movement damage to your hands and wrists. The longer you work on the same pad, the less effective that pad becomes as a work surface. Eventually it will need to be replaced.

On the other hand, the Clover Brush Mat does not give at all. The needles slip between the bristles so there is no damage to the needles, and neither does the surface give. Every poke is more efficient! The only downside to the brush mat is the fact that the bristles can and will "grab" fiber (but so will foam). This can be easily remedied by placing a piece of flannel over the mat. I have tried other fabrics for this purpose and flannel really seems to work best. The flannel will need to be replaced from time to time, but that is far less expensive than replacing a whole foam pad. I recommend using flannel of a neutral color that will differ in color to the fibers you use. Neutral colors make other colors stand out, thus making it easier to see the fibers with which you are working. The flannel may "beard" with continued use. "Bearding" is the process of some fibers getting stuck in the flannel. I usually pull them out if there are too many and have also used packaging tape to lift off such fibers.

The mat may need to be cleaned now and then. This is easily done with a very fine knitting needle, but there are some advantages to having at least some fiber stuck way down in the bristles. When you get to a point in a project where you are using pins to secure the object to the mat those fibers deep in the mat will help to hold your pins in place.

TOOLS for NEEDLES:

Many people find it uncomfortable to hold a needle for an extended period of time. There are a variety of multi-needle tools on the market but almost all of them are designed for flat felting and not sculpture. The exception is a pen like tool produced by Clover which can hold up to three needles. I personally don't like the pen shape. I've seen needles that have had the "L" dipped in liquid rubber to provide a more comfortable grip. I've seen two needles dipped together in the liquid rubber which may be useful until you break one of the needles. Dissatisfied with the multiple needle tools on the market I made my own. They are comfortable to hold for extended periods of time and each tool has multiple uses. I've found my tools to be so helpful that I made molds so that I could have duplicate tools fitted with different sized needles. I use a piece of dense foam to store my needles in tools when not in use.

OTHER TOOLS and ACCESSORIES:

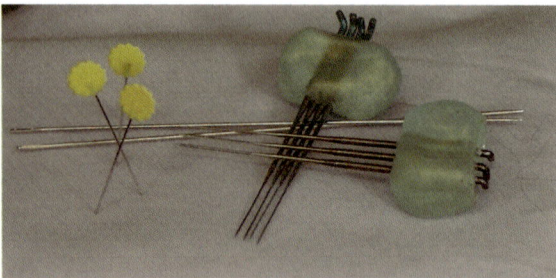

Pictured are some long pins, two of my own tools: the "four together" and the "three wide", and in the background long doll needles.

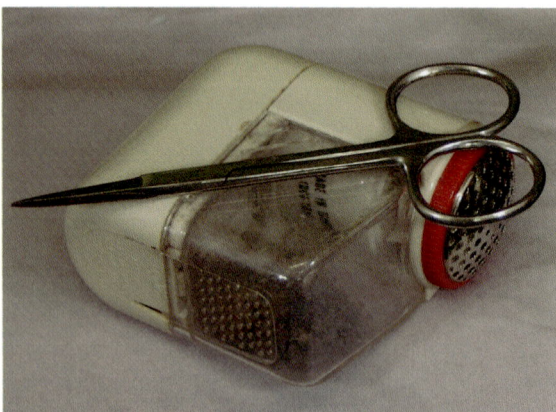

Here are scissors and a sweater shaver which are very useful tools for trimming stray fibers and to neaten your work.

Depending on the project you have in mind, you may need a variety of tools. Some that I find useful for doing sculptures of animals are:

Glass eyes:
There is a wide variety of quality in glass eyes and they can come with posts or without them. The best, most uniform quality I have found has been from taxidermy supply. I purchase mine without posts and glue on posts of my own to save expense. I've seen eyes needle felted out of wool and I've seen eyes made from polymer clay. If you like the look of those that can be a good way to go, I personally prefer the look of quality glass eyes.

Long pins:
Long pins are useful for pinning parts together temporarily to see how things are shaping up and for keeping a piece in place on the work surface for doing detailing.

Sewing and Bead Needles:
Long sharps and beading needles can be most useful when coupled with thread, floss and monofilament. Both types of needles can be used for a variety of purposes from adding whiskers, securing bead eyes, or adding other forms of embellishment.

Doll Needles:
These are very long sturdy needles and are excellent for starting thin cylinder shapes.

Wire:
Wire can be used for making armatures. It is best to use a non-rusting wire for this purpose. I will discuss armatures later in the book.

Glue:
I use glue to secure eyes and whiskers into place. Many artists do not glue their whiskers in place. Should you choose to not glue them do tell whoever buys your piece so they don't accidentally pull them out. You want to choose an acid free glue if you want your pieces to last.

Scissors:
Most of the time you will pull your fibers into the lengths you need, but there are times when you need to cut fiber or trim off the flyaway fibers that just refused to get felted down. For that final finishing, a battery operated sweater shaver can be great - just remember to not apply too much pressure or you'll start shaving your piece and not just the flyaway fibers.

Carding brushes (two):
Carding brushes or wire dog brushes are extremely useful for blending colors. I will demonstrate how to use these later in the book.

Good lighting:
This is a must!! Ott-lites and other full spectrum bulbs are very easy on the eyes for long periods of time. Such lights help you to see your colors accurately.

Paper towels and/or hand wipes:
These are useful for so many things from sopping up the blood or cleaning of the top of the glue tube before use.

Toothpicks:
Useful for applying the least amount of glue needed to secure eyes or whiskers in place. I actually use a bit of thin gauge wire for this purpose.

Pliers and Wire Cutters

Reference and inspiration material:
It is almost always useful to have some photographs around that in some way relate to your chosen project. If you are doing a needle felted sculpture of a real animal I suggest that you not only have many photos of that animal but also photos of its skeleton.

ERGONOMICS:

It is worth your while to set up a work station that conforms to some basics of ergonomics. Needle felting is time consuming so you want to be comfortable and not put unnecessary strain on your body. Your chair should be such that your legs, knees and feet make a comfortable 90 degree angle to the floor, unless you happen to sit on a high draftsman chair (as I do) in which case your feet should comfortably sit on the footrests of the chair. Your table should be at a height so that your arms when bent comfortably rest on its surface. Provide yourself with wrist rests should you need them!

TECHNIQUES:

Okay – we have the basic equipment out of the way and can get on to the fun!

You can make just about anything needle felting and I'm not here to tell you how to make a cute barn owl or a cupcake pin cushion. You have to decide what you want to make and probably if you are reading this you already have ideas on what you want to make, you just want to improve your skills! So let's get to it!!

Needle felting is rather like reversing an explosion. You start out with large fluffy quantities of fiber and through labor and patience you shrink it down to a solid form with the use of barbed needles. So why does this work? The fiber has small scales and when agitated together, either by the use of felting needles or other forms of agitation when wet felting, those scales lock together. Fiber that has been very thoroughly felted is very difficult to pull apart.

Remember, whatever shape you are making, to start out larger than you want the finished item to be. The process of needle felting will always shrink the object to a smaller size.

NEEDLING:

Look closely at your needle. The majority of the needle is cylindrical shank and only the tip is angular in shape and has barbs. Generally you will want to insert your needle into the fiber to the full depth of the angular portion. This gives all of the barbs a chance to do their work felting the fiber. You insert and remove the needle at the same angle to avoid breaking the tip. Most often, you needle towards the very center.

Your basic needling move is to thrust the needle straight into the fiber and then remove it.

ALWAYS REMOVE YOUR NEEDLE AT THE SAME ANGLE IN WHICH IT ENTERED THE FIBER!

More needles are broken by changing direction in mid-poke! As you go in, so shall you exit! You can change your angle to anything you might wish when the needle is outside the fiber but once it is in the fiber you must remove it at the same angle. Don't worry – this is easy to do.

"Deep Needling" and "Needling in place" is the process of inserting a needle so the whole tip is thrust deep into the fiber. "Needling in place" is the same movement as "Deep Needling" but the needle is not completely removed before reinserting it. This can be done a few times or a dozen times. The needle goes in and is not completely removed until you've done a number of thrusts. With each thrust the barbs will grab different strands of the fiber and help to felt the piece.

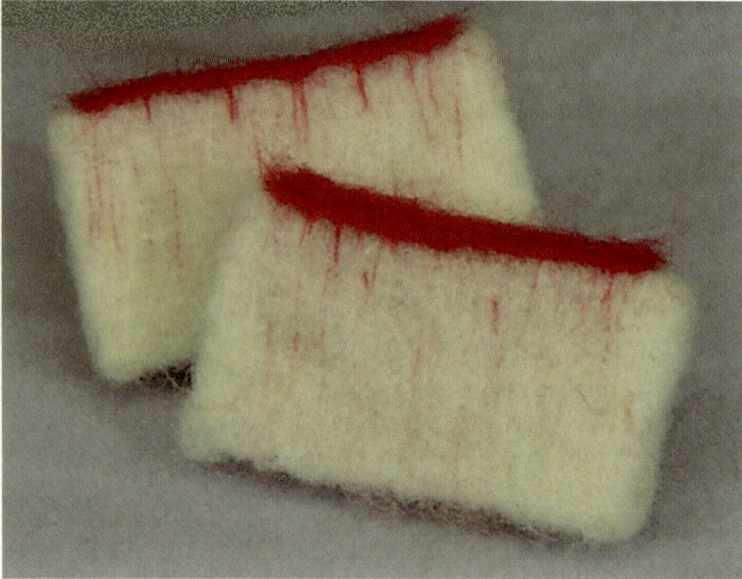

You can see in the photo above how the red fiber has been thrust deep into the previously felted white form. Deep felting is good but there are times when you may want or need to have a different approach.

While it would be impossible to pull all of the red fibers out as seen in the above photo, it would still be very possible to pull off all the surface red fiber. Only those fibers which have been embedded deeply in the white section would remain. To totally secure that top red fiber it would be necessary to continue needling in this manner for some time, but there are other ways to help secure that top fiber and make it far more resistant to being pulled away.

"Cross needling" is the process of needling your project at opposing angles so the point at which those thrusts intersect within the object forms roughly a 90 degree angle. The angle really isn't important so don't get in a tizzy over the 90 degrees, the point is to cause the fibers to be distributed and felted in a homogenous manner. Think of it as beating an egg. If you only do a limited amount of beating in one direction you will still have portions of the yolk and white that have not been thoroughly combined. If you beat (or needle your project) in a wide variety of directions and for a decent amount of time, you will have completely combined the yolk and the white and created a nice homogenous mixture (formed a more firmly felted piece).

To illustrate this clearly, I have only needled the red fiber in one specific direction and angle, and the blue in another. Now if you were to needle both the red and the blue at a lot of different angles and directions you would be forcing their fibers to lock into the form and become thoroughly felted.

The more you felt the better felted is your object AND if you are surface dressing (adding fiber to the top of a core) the more secure the layer will be.

Above I started with a sphere of white over which I laid and felted red fiber. I then covered that with white fiber, felted, covered that with blue fiber, felted and covered it all with a final layer of white and I felted that for good measure too.

The sphere above has been well felted. You can easily see that the different colored dressing fibers have been well distributed.

"Surface needling" is done at a very shallow angle to the core. Instead of needling towards the very middle, you needle to the side but you still want to insert the whole of the angular "working" portion of the needle. You might work across the dressed fiber needling in one direction, turn the piece and needle in the opposite direction, and then do a quarter turn and needle perpendicular to the first needling. The more directions you needle, all at that very shallow angle, the better!

Know where your barbs are! More specifically, know where the first barb is on your needle!

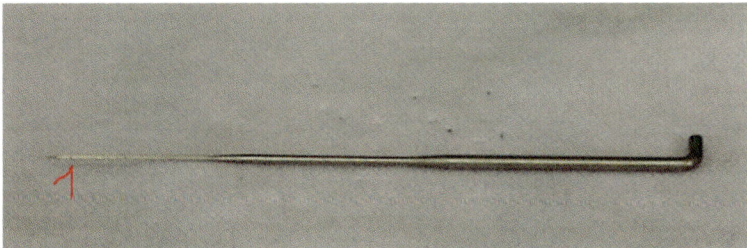

On the #42 needle picture above the first barb is on the same side as the turn in the "L" at the top of the needle. The first barb may be on the side or possibly even the front of another size or type of needle, but it is important for you to know where that first barb Is on YOUR needles. This is important information especially when you are needling at very shallow angles or when you are applying fur. You want that first barb to have the greatest opportunity to do the most good, which it does if that barb is the first to enter the fiber and facing the core or middle of your object.

When your core allows you room to felt deeply it is very easy to secure that dressed fabric. But what if your core isn't as thick as your needle's tip?

What if you know that your needle would poke out the other side? What does that do?

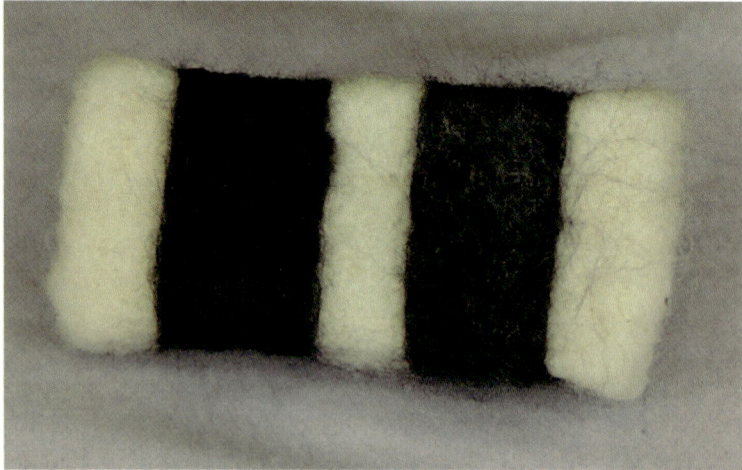

In the above photo I have dressed a white core with black fiber. The section on the left looks like pure black while the section on the right shows some white fibers from the core protruding through the black fiber. The section on the left was "surface needled" while the section on the right was deep needled completely through the core.

Tenacity

Chapter Three: Needling

Making a simple form:

SPHERE:

Take some fiber to start your sphere.
How much? It is impossible to measure fiber exactly so pull off as much as you think you might need. You may be wrong but it is a simple process to add or remove fiber.

Compress the fibers with your finger tips trying to form a rough sphere and while still holding the fiber begin to needle the fiber.

BE CAREFUL! Needles are SHARP!!!

Once your fiber holds a rough sphere shape, you will not need to continue compressing it with pressure from your fingers. Just hold and needle. Remove the needle completely, rotate the sphere a bit and needle again, evenly around the surface.

Repeat! Repeat! Repeat!

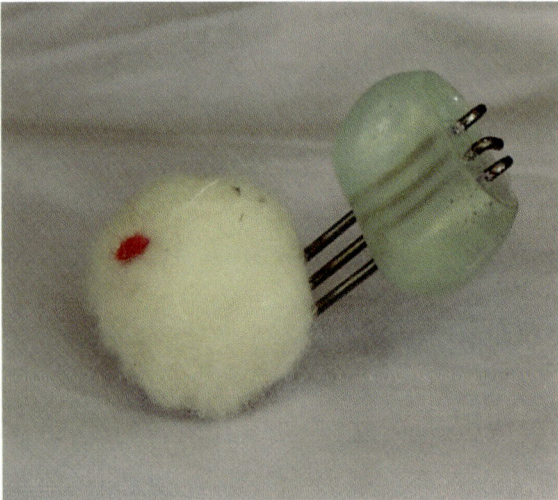

I've added a red dot to this demo sphere in an attempt to make the directions more clear.

While it is always a good idea to do some DEEP needling, a lot can be accomplished with some good surface needling thrown in too.

After I've got my sphere started I begin a process of needle, roll, needle and roll all the way around the sphere.

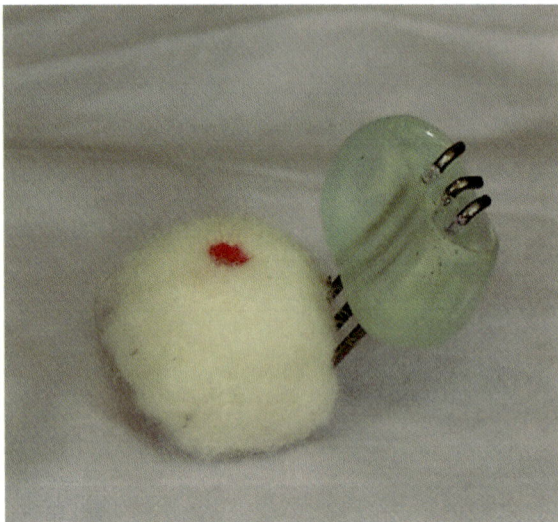

I'll needle and roll in one direction and then I will turn the sphere and needle and roll again. Because I have turned the sphere I am actually needling in a different direction.

So deep needle, needle and roll and deep needle again.

You will probably find a method of doing this that works well for you and that is just as it should be.

The goal is to make your sphere as uniformly round as is possible.

If one area bulges out more than does another area, needle it!!

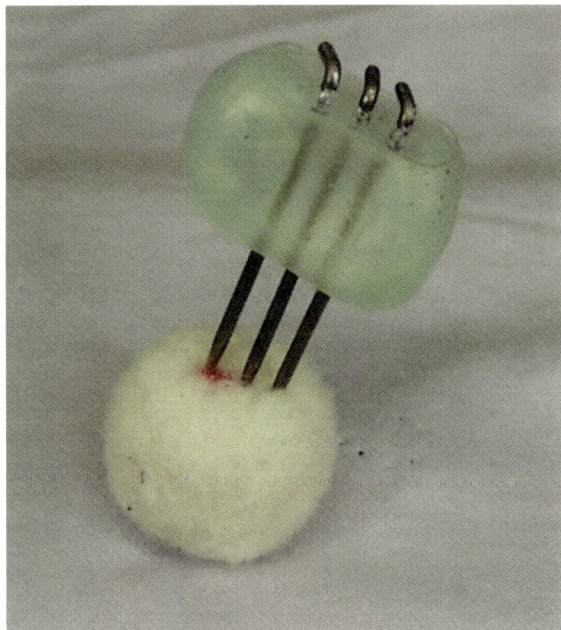

Don't be surprised when what looked like a lot of fiber has felted down into a sphere that is smaller than you anticipated and smaller than you need or want.

If the sphere isn't large enough, add more fiber!

Now you can take a long bit of fiber and wrap it around the sphere over and over – rather like winding a ball of yarn. Or you can add smaller quantities of fiber and needle them in as you go until you have a sphere that is just the size you wanted.

EGG:

Take some fiber and roll it into a basic egg shape.

The tighter you roll the fiber the less over all felting you will need to do, but you will still need to do a lot as I will demonstrate later.

Felt uniformly all over, rotating and turning your egg as you needle.

Continue to rotate and turn and needle as the egg becomes smaller and smaller and more firmly felted.

This egg could have easily been reduced in size but I decided to use this medium firm egg to demonstrate how you can transform one shape into another. That demonstration will follow in a later chapter.

CUBE/box: (oh, alright this isn't precisely a cube but it does demonstrate how it is done)

Take some fiber (yes, whatever you think is going to be about the right amount). With experience you will get better at judging how much fiber you will need.

I'm using a core fiber here and I've pulled off a length that is about three times as long as it is wide.

I start out by folding it into thirds which make for a very fluffy, roughly box shaped pile of fiber.

I begin by needling that exposed end into the fiber below.

I very gently needle on all six sides of my fiber to make it look more like a box.

When creating more complex shapes it is best to go slowly and lightly with your needling.

Keep rotating and working all sides of your form.

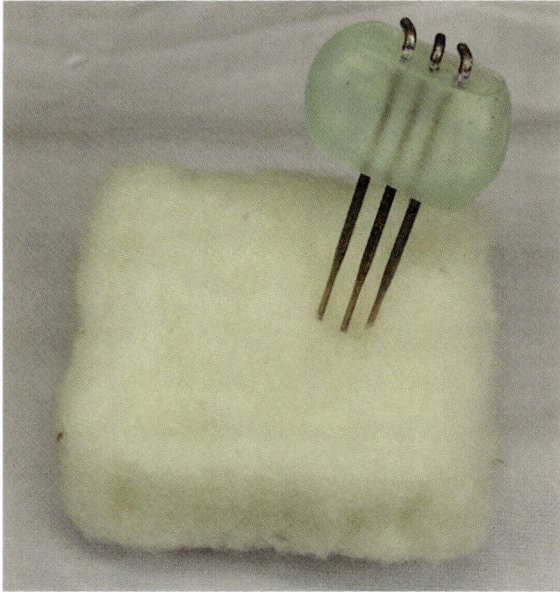

If you needle too hard and too quickly, your form will start to distort and you will have difficulty felting the fiber down into the form you really want.

So far on this sample piece I have been working with my "three needles wide" tool fitted with #38 star needles.

All of this work could be done by a single needle but it would take a lot more time than it would with multiple needle tools.

I have two of my tools pictured with the box which has shrunk further in size. The tools are the "three needles wide" with the #38 star needles and the "four together" fitted with #42 needles.

I used both tools to felt the box down to this size.

As you can see, the box gets smaller and smaller the more I gently needle it, always working all sides of the box!

This box has rounded corners, and with fiber it would not be possible to get sharp corners although you could get very close. To do so, more attention would need to be paid to better define the corners.

I continued to felt the box even smaller, always turning and working all sides uniformly so now it is a very firm little box shaped object.

The importance of rotating and needling the object evenly:

I'm temporarily interrupting the discussion of making basic three dimensional shapes to stress how very important it is to keep the shape in mind and to rotate, turn and needle the object evenly.

If this fiber is meant to be a cube or a brick and you needle mostly on the two large sides the result will not be a brick, the result will be a thick rectangle, so rotate and turn your object often when needling.

Yoga

LOG/Cylinder:

Take a length of fiber (this is core fiber) and roll it up. The tighter you roll it the less felting you will need to do but you will still need to do quite a bit.

You should start with a rolled log <u>longer</u> than you want your finished log to be.

Start needling the log from all sides including the ends. Needle and roll and rotate and needle some more.

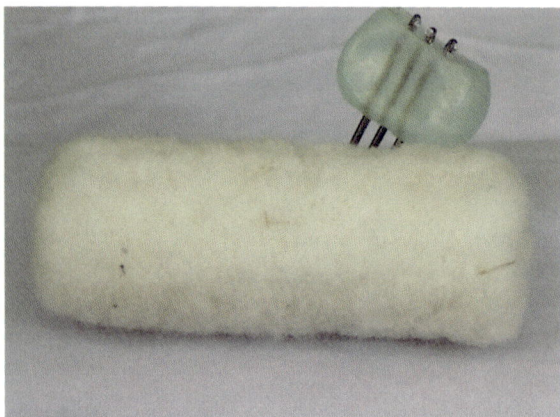

The log will gradually compact and get smaller and firmer as you continue to felt.

Continue to felt the log until it is firmly felted.

It is easier to add to the diameter of your log than it is to add to the length of your log.

If you needed this log to be thicker, just add another layer.

If you really need it to be longer – try rolling it between your hands very firmly and even try pulling it to be longer. You can also add fiber to the ends but that is a bit more awkward – it still will probably work out well in the end. Fiber and needle felting are very forgiving.

The above technique for making a log/cylinder is useful for making a log of most sizes but is not the best technique for making a thin log/cylinder. Later I will show you a good way to make a thin cylinder but first let's discuss:

Wrapping:

Wrapping fiber around a piece of wire or some other structure is not felting. Wrapped fibers can be secured so that they will stay wrapped but they are still not felted. Felting adds strength and structure.

The fiber on the left has been surface felted to the cylinder. Normally I would also deep felt this fiber, but for the purposes of this demonstration surface felting was enough.

The same fiber wrapped in two places around a well felted cylinder.

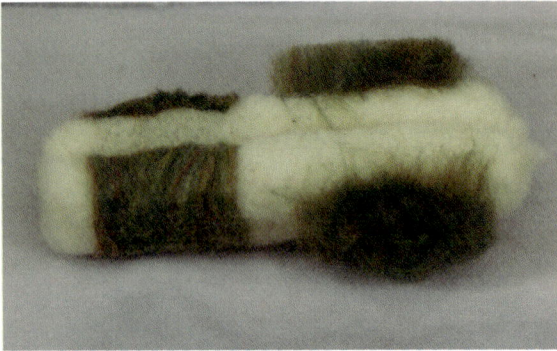

That same cylinder cut.

Notice that the fiber which has at least had a fair amount of surface felting stays in place. It has become part of the cylinder and adds some strength to the whole

The wrapped fiber on the right completely falls away; it has provided no strength to the whole. While it may be unlikely that a wrapped object would be cut in such a manner the consequences of even a small cut would be the same.

Wrapping fiber is quite often a very good way to get a cylindrical piece started, but to be felted properly and firmly, all signs of it starting out as a wrapped piece should disappear.

Thin Cylinder:

Now let's take a look at wrapping a thin cylinder. In the following photos I am using some core fiber, wrapped around a doll needle, to start the thin cylinder.

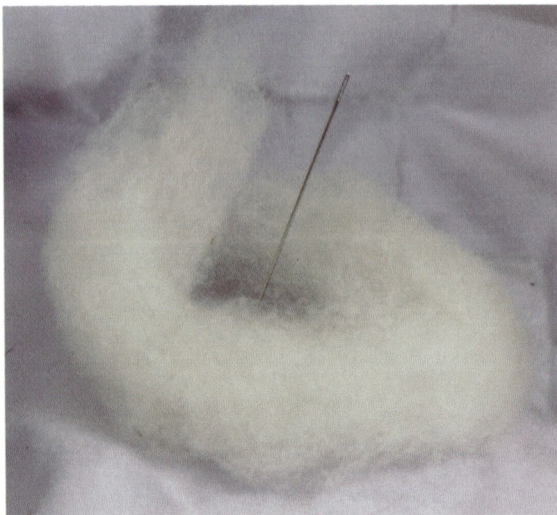

Why use core fiber? Aside from the fact that you will save some of your more expensive fibers for the exterior, a core fiber can add additional strength to a thin cylinder and will be easier to felt firmly than would be a fine fiber such as Merino, so there is structural strength added as well as saving you some time.

The downside is that when you continue to felt the thin cylinder firmer and firmer, some of that core fiber is going to be poking through your "dressing" fiber. These core fibers can be redressed later.

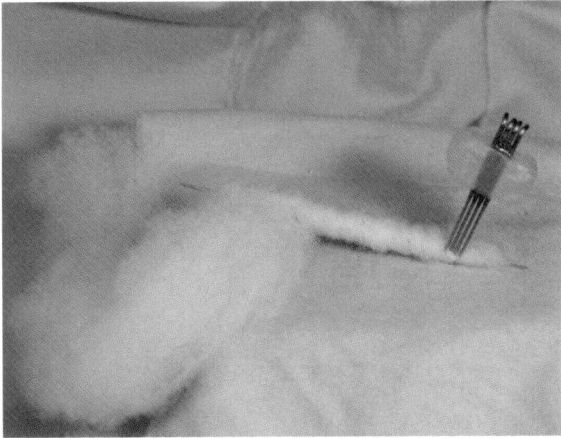

The core fiber has been wrapped around the doll needle and needled (with one of my four together needle tools) to secure it and to begin felting its shape.

As with an armature you need to be careful of the doll needle in the middle. Needle as close to it as possible but avoid hitting it. Unlike an armature wire which would stay inside the piece, the doll needle will be removed later.

Uh oh! I have too much core fiber! What do I do? What do I do?

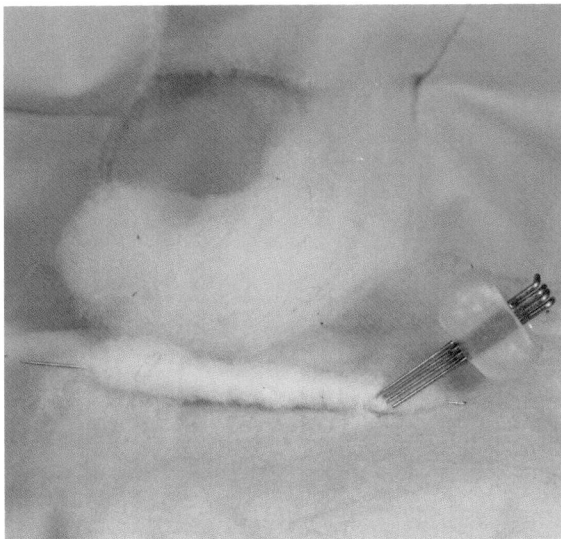

Cut or pull off the excess fiber.

I've heard from other needle felters that you should never cut your fiber. This isn't exactly true. The problem with cut fiber is you have all these fibers ending at the same spot whereas when you pull fiber off you will have some fibers be short and some longer making it easier to felt away the signs that you removed excess fiber.

There are times when cutting the fiber won't matter or is a wiser choice.

Chapter Four: Simple Forms

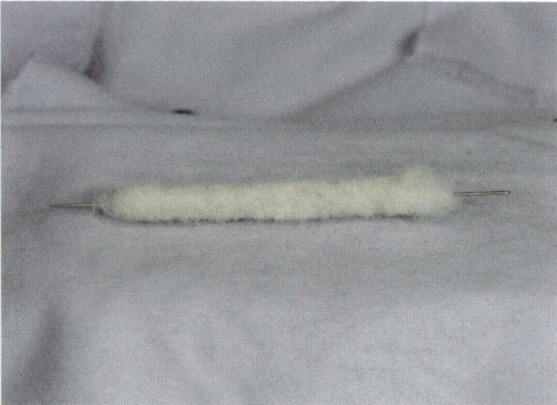

Continue to needle carefully around the central doll needle to form a nicely felted cylinder.

Larger needles are more efficient for doing your initial felting. As a piece becomes more firmly felted, you may wish to switch to finer needles.

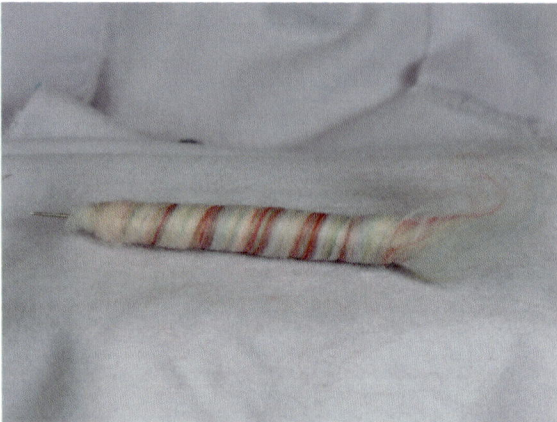

Wrapping the dress fiber: I've chosen to use a striped fiber for these photos because it more clearly demonstrates the level of felting as the needling progresses.

At this point I could just secure the loose ends and call it done, but it is very obvious that the cylinder is only wrapped and not felted. It is structurally not as sound as a felted piece.

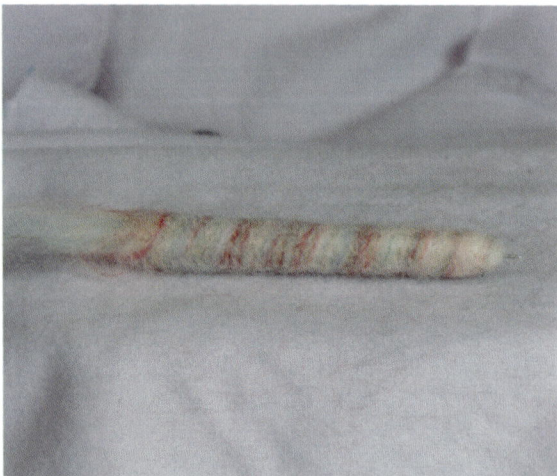

Here I have done some needling and you can see that the stripes are beginning to be less distinct.

This is superior to a merely wrapped cylinder but we can do better.

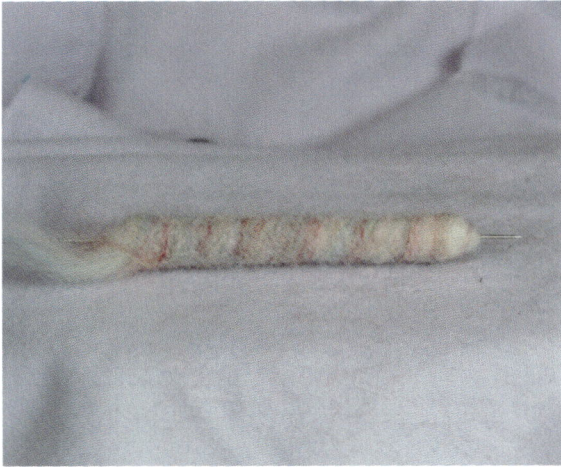

Here the cylinder has been needled even further and while the stripes are still visible because of the fiber I chose, it is clear that the over all cylinder is much more firmly felted.

I could obscure the stripes further by doing some angle felting. Instead of needling perpendicular to the cylinder, needling at various angles will cause the stripes to become less distinct.

At this point the cylinder is well enough established so that the doll needle can be removed and even more needling can be done to firm the cylinder.

When the doll needle is removed we end up having the space that the doll needle occupied as a "hole" in the felted form. It won't really stay a hole as the fiber will expand to fill in that space previously occupied by the doll needle but what is important is that area will not be firmly felted. This "hole" needs to be removed by additional felting, and because the doll needle is no longer there occupying its own physical space, the cylinder upon which we have been working will get smaller in diameter. Additional dressing fiber can be added to the exterior to compensate for the reduction in diameter.

If you intend to manipulate the shape of the cylinder it is best to keep it at medium firmness.

You can taper a thin cylinder by carefully controlling the thickness of the fiber.

Caramel

Stuffing the Tube:

You can stuff additional fiber into the middle of a cylinder by inserting it from one end or the other and inserting the needle deep into the middle.

Work with small amounts of fiber and get them well felted in before adding more.

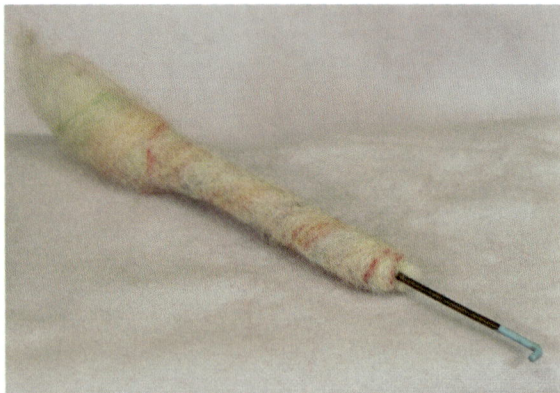

Adding fiber in this manner can help to strengthen the cylinder as a whole.

Fiber can be stuffed in to more than just cylinders, and doing so can help lessen the shrinking that happens when needling the exterior of an object while simultaneously increasing the objects over all firmness.

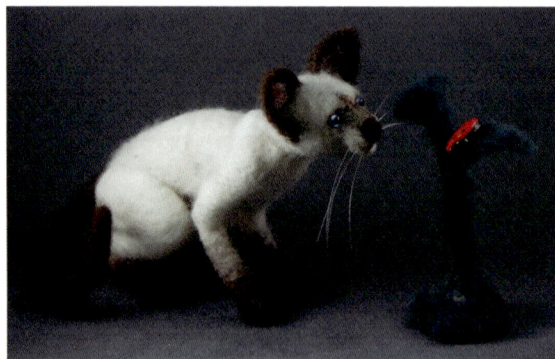

Ming

How firmly should you needle felt your project?

This is really a two part question.

The first part is: "How firm does your object need to be while a work in progress?" and the second is: "How firm should your finished object be?"

Firmness of a work in progress:

An object that is medium firm allows for manipulation of the fibers/object. It is possible to make a work in progress very firm, but the techniques that you will use to make your finished project may be considerably different than if your fiber/object still has some "give".

Firmness of a finished project:

That depends on the nature of your project and its intended "life". If you are making a needle felted dryer ball, the purpose of which is to help dry and fluff clothes in the dryer, you don't need to make it super firm. If you are making a sculpture of a bull that you want to be enjoyed for generations, and into which you are investing a lot of your time and talent, you want the piece to be firm. It is still pretty much a personal and artistic call.

Any portion of your project which is going to support additional portions of your project should be very firmly felted.

This may seem pretty obvious but it is worth emphasizing. If you are making an animal that is standing, the legs need to be strong enough to support the body.

Poppet

How firm is firm:

This is obviously a very difficult quality to describe.

A "medium firm" object will feel fairly solid but will be easy to needle without a great deal of force. As shown in following photos, a medium firm object is relatively easy to manipulate. It will have a sort of spongy feel. You can compress it with the force of your fingers but it will spring back into shape.

A "very firm" object will feel heavier and require a bit of force to needle further. Manipulation of a "very firm" object is possible but will require a lot more effort and it would probably be easier to add on fiber to make changes rather than to attempt to change the existing form.

An "extremely firm" object will be very dense and needling it further will be very difficult. Changes to the appearance/shape of an "extremely firm" object are almost always done by addition or subtraction rather than manipulation.

It remains a very real possibility that what I may define as being "medium firm" you might define as being "very firm". It really doesn't matter. What does matter is developing an understanding of the integrity of your objects and what works best for you. I have made objects that I considered finished and months later upon examining them again decided that some parts were not firmly felted enough so I did additional felting.

Time and experience are the best teachers.

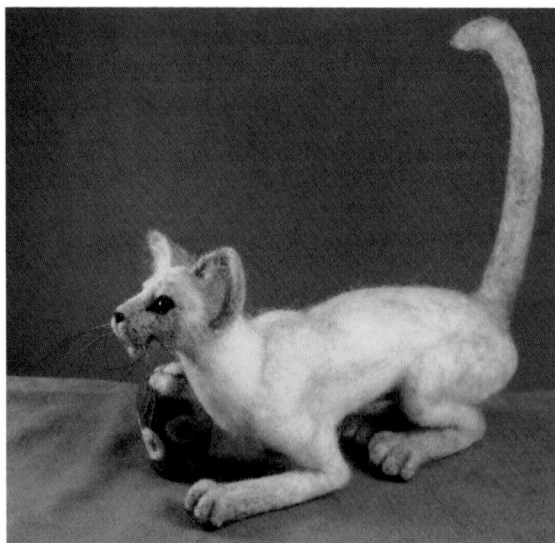

Latte

Chapter Five: Firmness

MANIPULATING AN OBJECT:

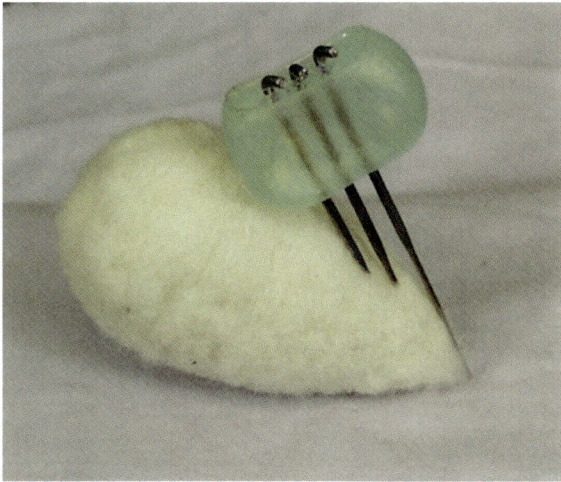

An egg can be transformed into a cone.

First we want to make the narrower end of the egg and turn it into a tip. This is done by concentrated "Directional Needling".

As seen in the photo the needles are forcing that previously rounded end out and by needling and rotating the egg shape while keeping the needles always pointing in the direction we want the alteration of shape a point is created.

"Directional Needling" –
Needling in the direction of the desired alteration.

Needle in the fiber from that bottom area to flatten the bottom.

The former egg looks a lot more like a cone.

Had the egg been super firm it would have been very difficult to make this transformation and probably would have required the addition of a lot of fiber to create a point and to create a flat bottom.

The cone would have most likely ended up being larger than the original egg.

It is perfectly possible to start out just to make a cone without making an egg first. It would also be possible to turn a cone into an egg.

An egg can be transformed into a pear shaped object. A short fat cylinder can be transformed into a truncated cone shape. Fiber can be added to the ends of a cylinder to make it a barbell. The possibilities are endless. Simple forms can be transformed into more complex forms.

There isn't a right or a wrong way to do these things. What is important is to find the method that works best for you.

Pumpkin

There are other ways to manipulate an object.

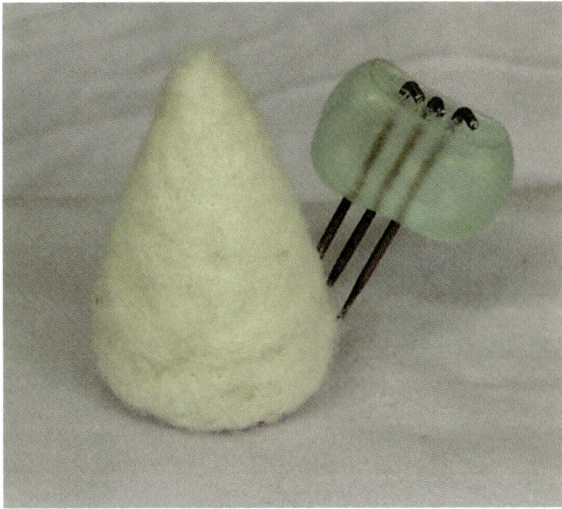

Here's the basic cone shape that we previously made.

With additional effort we could flatten that bottom even more and make it a perfect cone rather than this slightly rounded bottomed cone.

We can also do other things with it given that over all we're still dealing with a medium firm object.

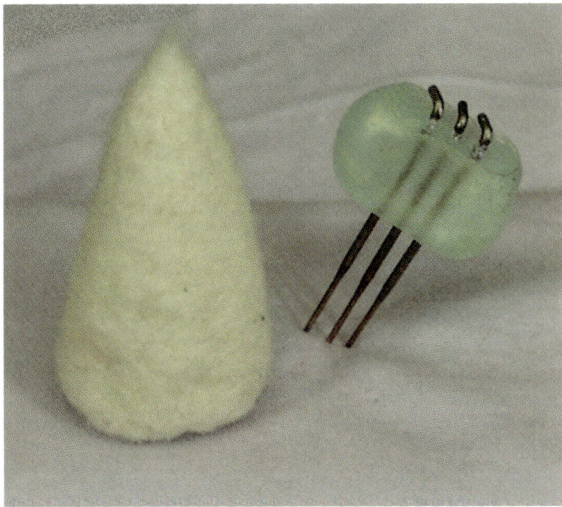

To make it taller I have pulled on it and rolled it firmly between my palms.

If I continued to do that I could make it even taller and narrower.

The force of your fingers and hands can manipulate basic forms very effectively.

It also can be manipulated in other ways.

Medium firm objects are very malleable. You can make a lot of changes to a medium firm object that would be far more difficult if not impossible to make to a very firm object.

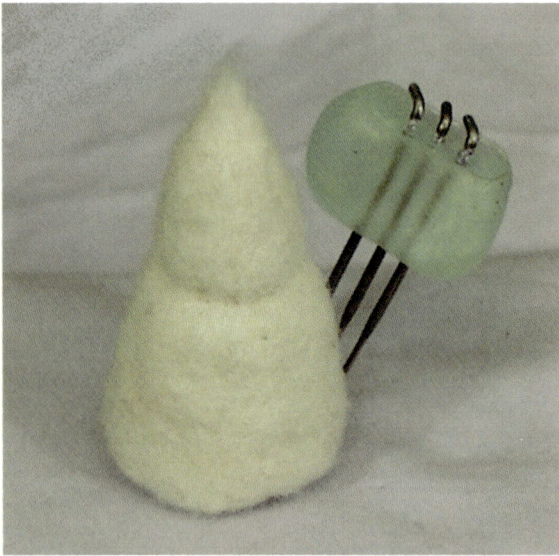

Needling repeatedly around the cone near the tip end creates a different shape.

Needling perpendicular lines from the base to the previous indentation creates a pleasing effect.

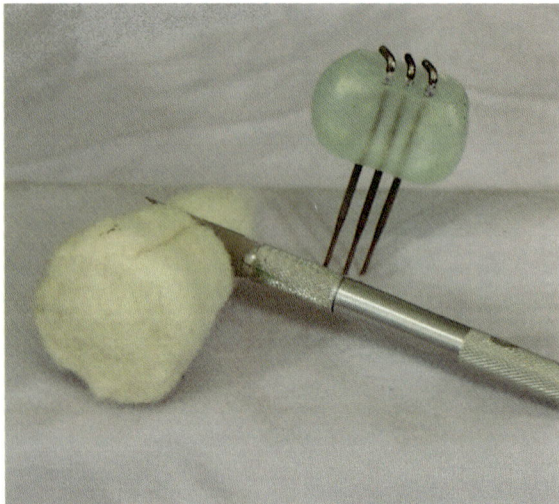

But maybe we don't want that tip any more.

Cut it off.

There are two objects now both of which could be very useful!

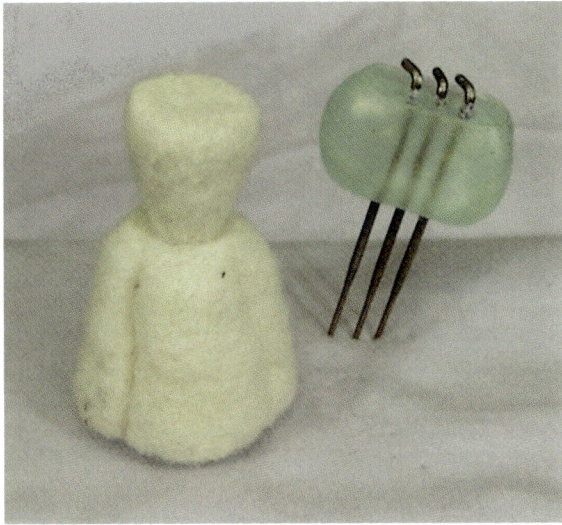

Or maybe they'd be useful put back together but not as they were originally.

Here I just made a couple small slits and used a knitting needle to make a hole for the inverted top to be positioned on the bottom piece.

The top was then felted into the bottom piece.

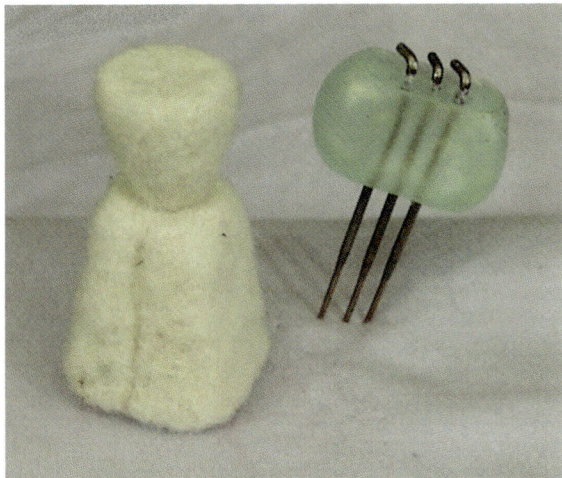

Maybe the sides should be flatter.

Maybe they should be flattened even more.

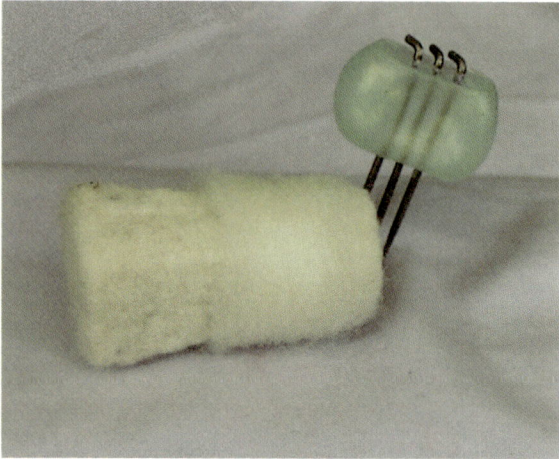

Add some fiber.

Felt that all together.

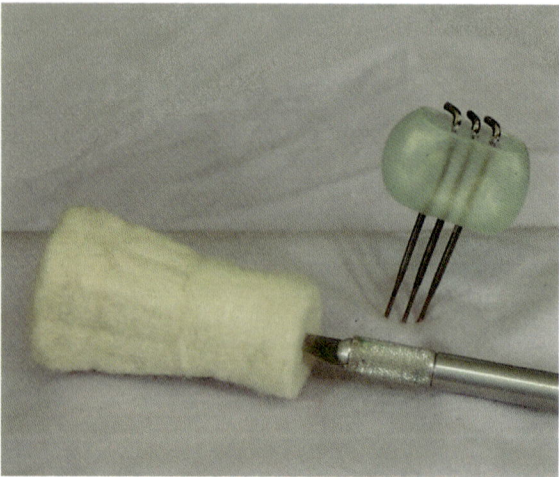

Maybe the top should be flared but that area has been felted pretty well so a few shallow cuts in the middle will assist.

By needling and turning and needling more the top can begin to take on a flare.

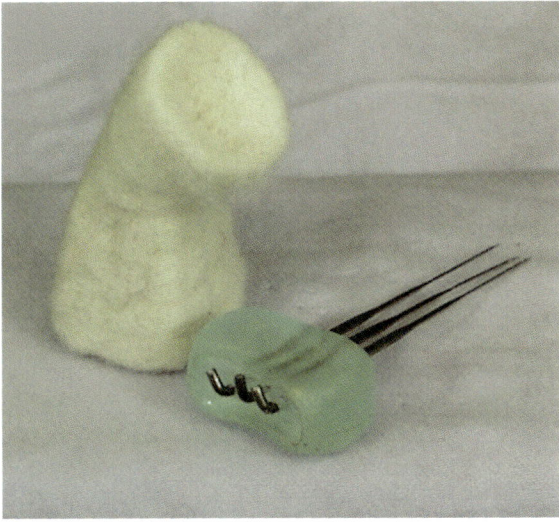

Bend it and needle to preserve the bend that you created with the pressure of your fingers.

Bend and needle and bend it even more – whatever you want.

With an object that is medium firm in nature you can manipulate it in a great many ways with the use of your fingers, hands and needles.

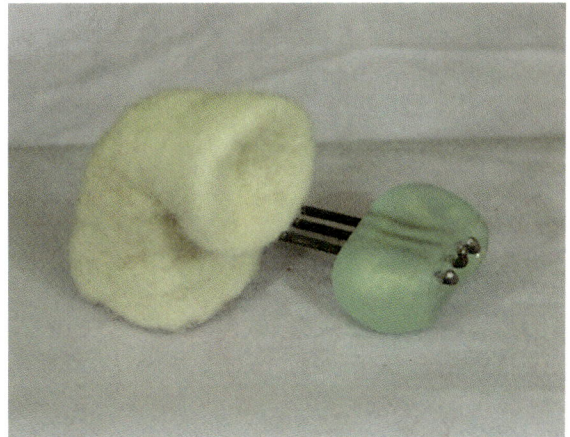

Theo

COMBINING SIMPLE FORMS:

Cone added on to a Sphere:

Take some fiber.

Now in this example I am using some "dressing" fiber.

This new fiber is laid out in roughly a circle shape on the work surface.

Using needles, concentrate most of the fiber to the center of the circle. You will still want some fluffy outer bits of fiber but you want most of that fiber to be in the middle.

Needle this a bit so it will hold this shape.

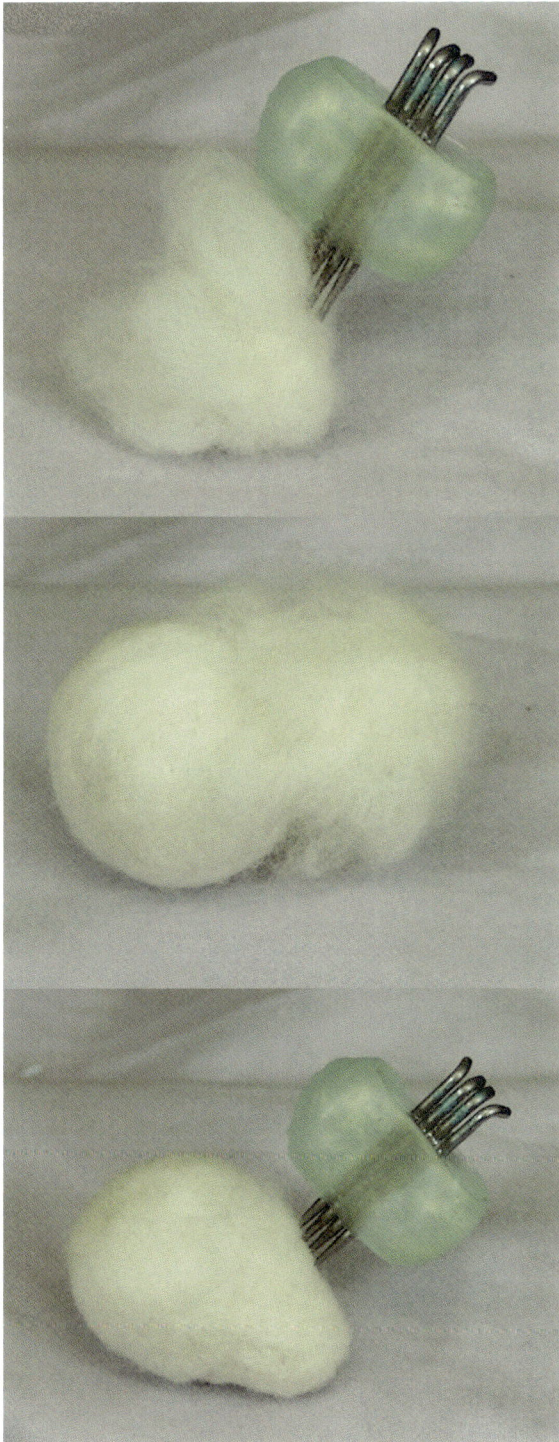

Next, lift up the edge of your circle of fiber and fold it over itself. Needle the fiber gently at the thick center in this fold. Gently rotate your fiber from that thick center and (keeping it folded) and needle that thick center some more. Rotate and needle again until you have a roughly fat cone. The edges will have a little bit of fiber, and the fat tip will have a lot.

That is just how we want it to be!

Place the fat cone against your sphere and needle it in place. You will need to rotate the sphere and needle along the loose edge of the fat cone all the way around the sphere.

You may notice that in this photo I have secured the fat cone not to the middle of the sphere but to one side. That will be clearer in the next photograph.

I've done a lot more needling to secure the fat cone to the sphere. The fat cone should clearly appear to be on just one side of the sphere.

Gosh – doesn't that look like it might be the shape of a dog head? Or maybe it looks like a skull of a human, or the beginning of an ice cream cone, or an egg.

My point is that by combining two simple shapes, we can make a more complex shape that can allow us to make anything we want!

Chapter Seven: Combining Simple Forms

"But you already showed me how to make an egg. Why use this more complex method to arrive at the same end result?"

I demonstrated this more complex method because they are <u>not</u> the same end result.

When you create an egg shape you end up with an egg that should be pretty <u>evenly</u> firm through out the whole object. When you combine two objects such as a sphere and a cone you can control how firm each portion is separately. The sphere in this combined example is much more firmly felted than is the cone that was applied.

If, in whatever project you have in mind, you do not intend to manipulate greatly one portion of a combined object (in this example: the sphere) but do intend to manipulate the other (the cone) the differences in firmness will assist you.

Wixie – my husband's Pritten

Creating "flat" shapes:

Oval: truncated (i.e. one end will not be felted)

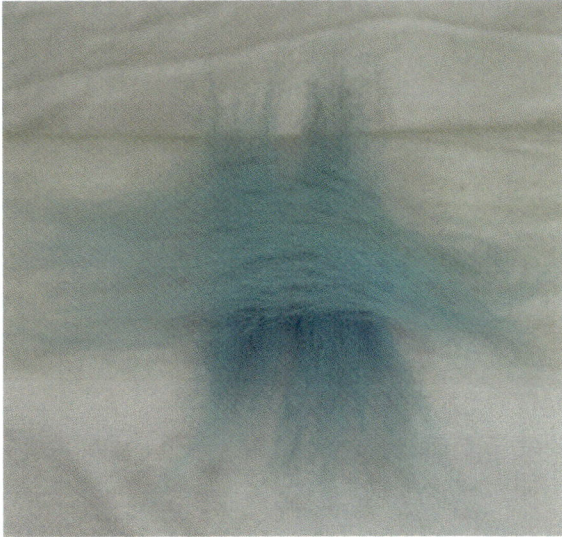

On your work surface, lay out some fiber longer than you want your finished oval to be on your work surface. Place some additional fiber crosswise over the first layer of fiber. This second layer should be wider than you want the finished width to be but not significantly wider or you will have too much fiber.

Why lay out two layers like this?

Fibers that are all laid out in one direction are difficult to felt because the needles can just slip through and not connect with other fibers. By laying some fiber crosswise, the needles and fibers have an easier time felting together.

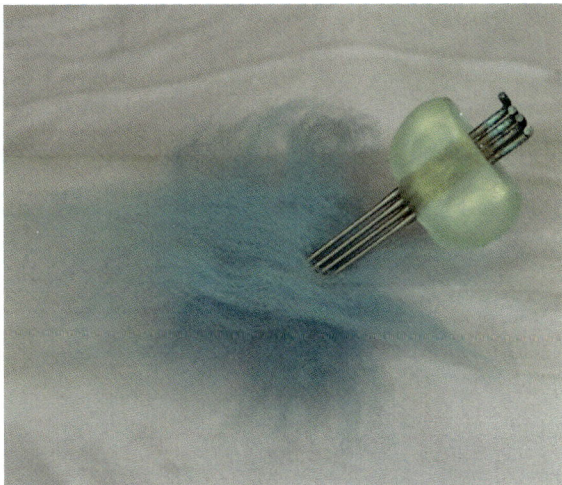

These are relatively thin layers of fiber, so when you pick the whole up to felt from the other side, do so carefully or the delicate structure will fall apart on you.

Some of the fibers are most likely stuck in the work surface and will resist being picked up to turn the whole piece over.

Just be prepared for this and turn the fibers over gently.

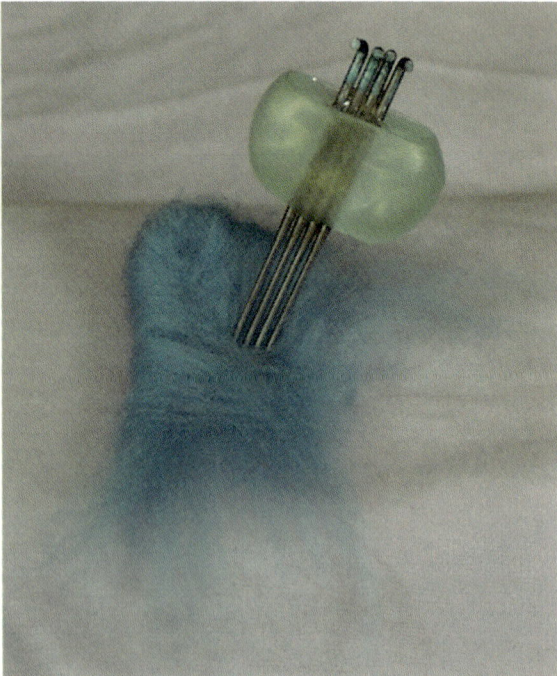

Begin to bring in the edges to start forming the oval. Felt the folded in fibers into the central area that you previously felted.

Once the edges are folded in, try to keep the thickness of the fiber as uniform as possible. This is a bit more difficult at the tips where you are folding the whole rounded edge of fiber towards the center, but it will work.

TURN THE FLAT PIECE OVER OFTEN.

If you felt too long on one side, you risk felting the piece into the flannel or whatever fabric you have covering your work surface.

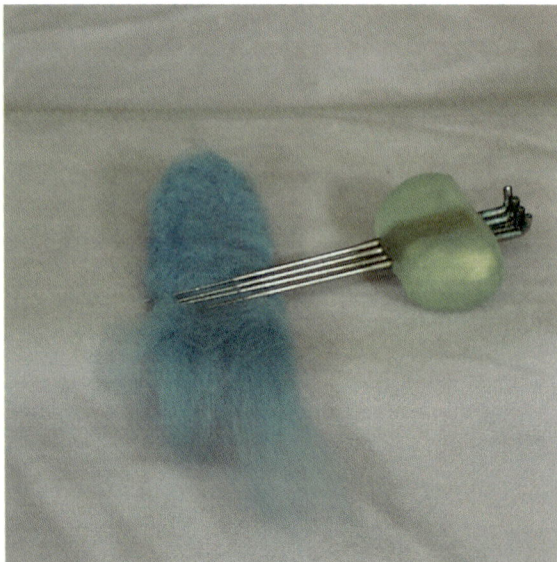

Continue to fold in the fiber from the other side to really establish that truncated oval. Felt well on both sides.

You want to do deep felting which will no doubt result in some of your fiber getting stuck in your work surface. That's okay.

You will also want to so some surface felting, working the needles at very shallow angles and in lots of directions.

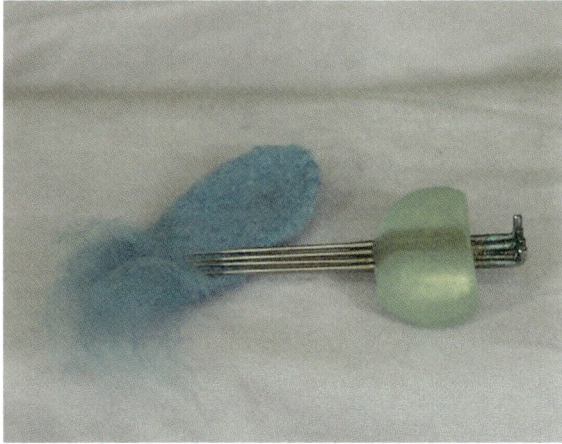

Continue to felt both deep and surface turning the oval over and working both sides until it is firmly felted.

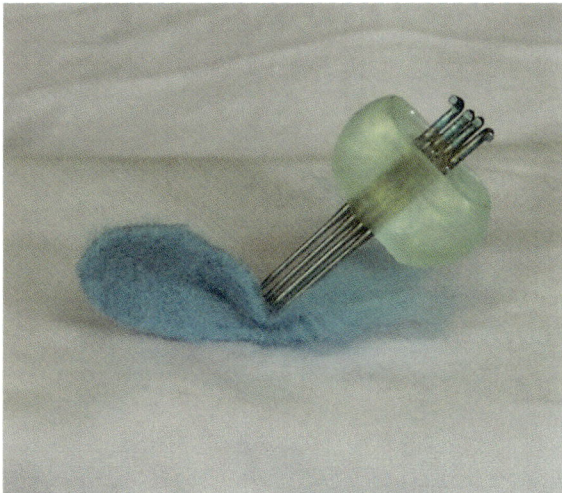

Flat felted pieces can be manipulated by folding and felting the fold.

They can also be shaped by needling where you want to curve the oval while your fingers gently encourage the edges to curl up.

Can you see how that might be useful?

Princess

Triangle:

As with the oval, start out by laying out some fiber. For a triangle you want to lay your longer fiber side to side.

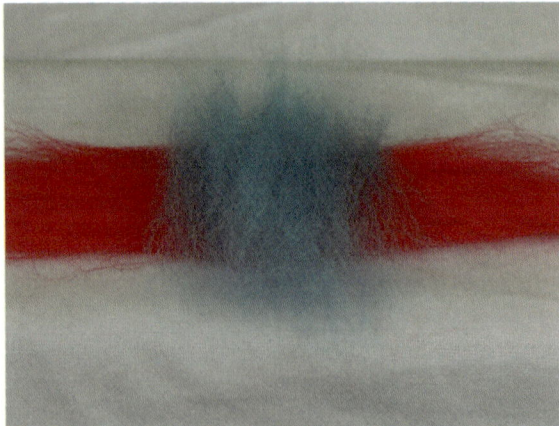

Lay some shorter fiber crosswise over the first layer to encourage felting.

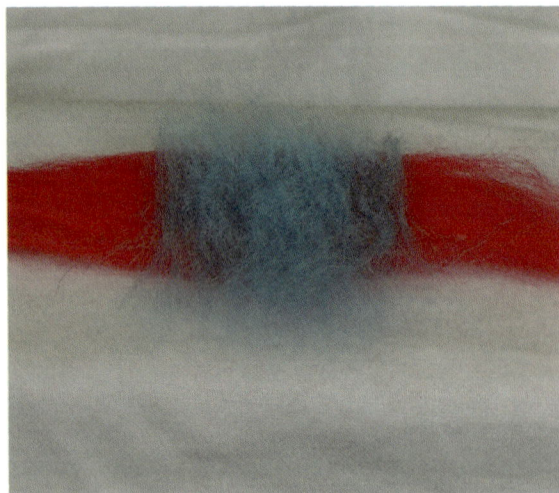

Felt these two layers together and remember that when you go to turn them over that their structure at this point is rather delicate. Handle it gently.

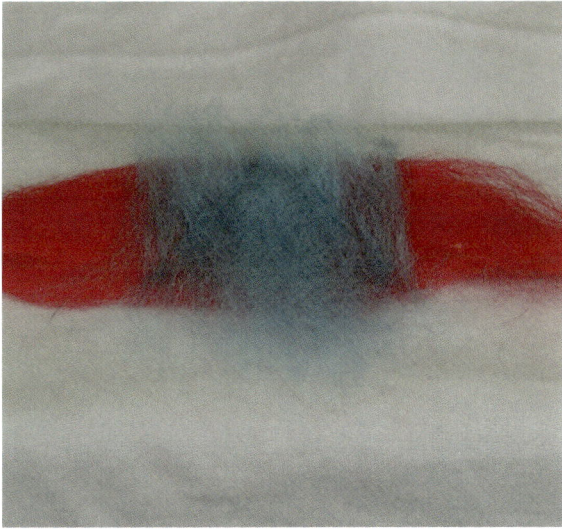

Needle the shape of two sides of a triangle into the fibers. The angle should be roughly 45 degrees from the top edge.

Truthfully you can make a triangle with any angle you want. It doesn't need to be 45 degrees but this is the easiest proportion for learning to make a flat felted triangle.

Fold in one side of the fiber along one of the triangular side lines you needled in the previous step.

Needle that into place, both deep and surface needling but do not turn it over yet!

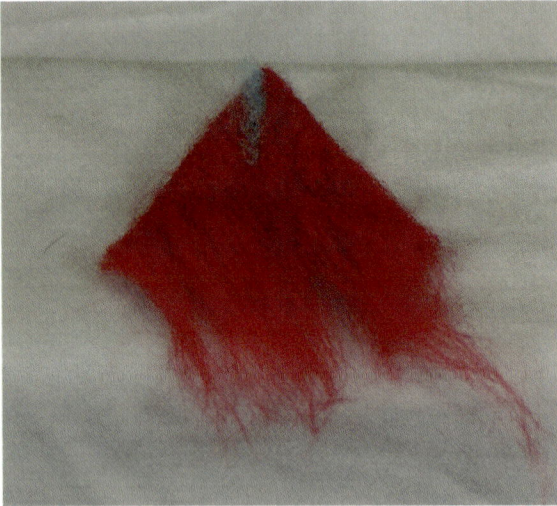

Now fold in the other side and needle it into the rest using both deep and surface needling.

Gently turn the piece over and needle from the other side.

TURN THE FLAT PIECE OVER OFTEN.

Repeat both deep and surface needling on both sides until your triangle is nicely felted.

You can tell when the fiber is nicely felted when it has a strong feel to it and is resistant to distortion.

Now if this furry edged triangle were going to be attached to some other shaped object for some reason, you may wish to be able to distort it a bit.

If, however, you wanted a pristine triangle that was really going to hold its shape you could fold in the last furry side and felt, felt and felt until it was as firm as you can make it.

There are many things you can do with your triangle. For example, the bottom of the triangle can be left with loose fibers to assist in felting it to another object, or they could be folded in to create a triangle with three smooth sides. The fibers can be folded in to form a curved side transforming the triangle into a leaf. The triangle can be cut; any flat felted piece can be cut as need directs. If you do not wish the cut to fray, then make certain that your flat felted piece is well felted prior to cutting. Cut only when need demands!

Free form flat felting:

Perhaps you want an odd shaped flat felted piece. These are as easy to create as the oval and the triangle I have already demonstrated.

Start with some carded fiber*. Lay the fiber out roughly in the shape you desire. Try to keep the fibers of an even thickness.

* carding fiber is illustrated in the section on blending fibers.

Lightly felt the fibers.

Start folding in the edges and lightly felting them in place, keeping the thickness of the fiber even as possible. Should you find that you have much too much fiber in one area for the shape you have in mind, you can gently pull off some of the excess fiber.

Continue gently folding in the edges and lightly felting until you have the shape you desire.

Once you have the shape you want, felt one side, turn the piece over and felt the other side and repeat that process until it is very nicely felted.

Using a mold to felt flat pieces:

Any cookie cutter that is open on both sides can be used as a flat felt mold.

If you are going to felt a very thin flat piece, the cookie cutter does not need to be very deep.

It is possible with deeper cookie cutters to felt three dimensional objects.

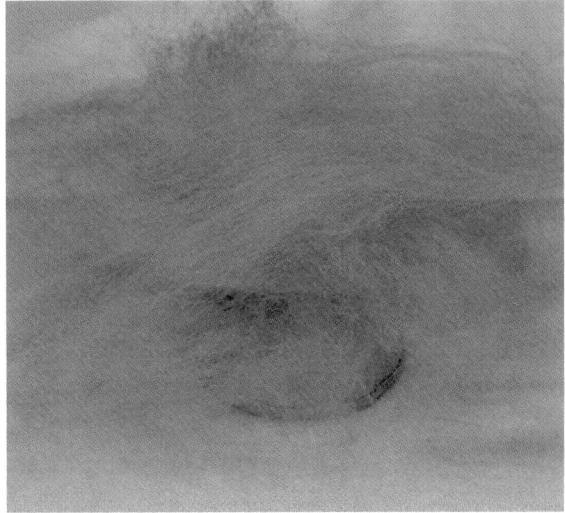

Pull off fiber a bit wider than your mold and lay it in all directions across the top of the mold or cookie cutter.

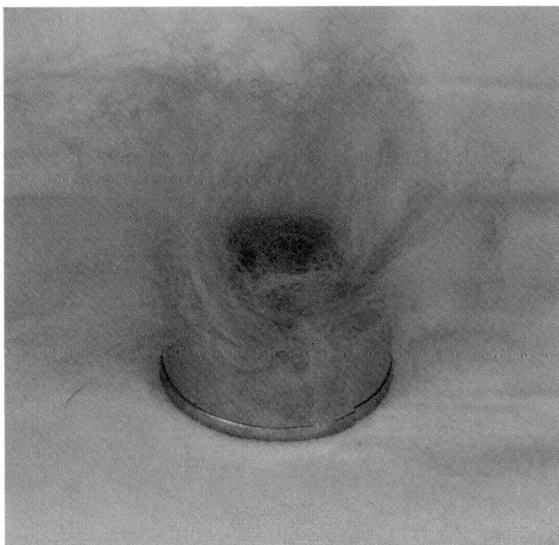

Push the fiber in the middle down into the mold.

Next, fold in the remaining fiber and stuff it down into the mold.

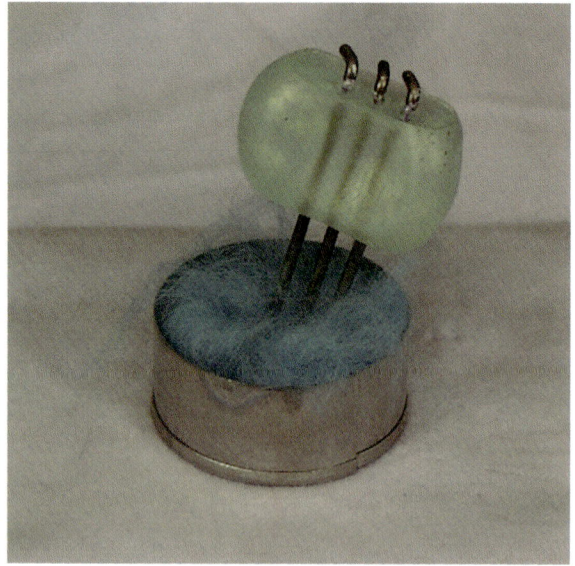

Begin to needle the fiber, being particularly carefully when needling around the edges of the mold.

Continue to felt the fibers in the mold.

Remove the mold and turn the flat felted piece over.

Chapter Eight: Creating Flat Shapes

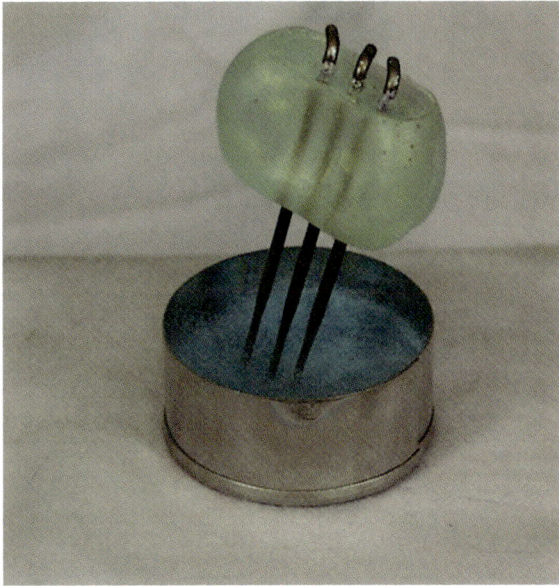

Insert the now turned-over piece back into the mold and felt well.

If your mold/cookie cutter is not symmetrical you will need to turn over both the mold and the felted piece.

Once the piece has been fairly well felted inside the mold, take it out and felt it without the mold.

TURN THE FLAT PIECE OVER OFTEN.

If you are using a mold that is irregular in shape lay out your fibers carefully so that when pushed into the mold and felted, all areas of the mold will be evenly filled. When necessary you can add extra fiber to fill any area you might have missed. Extra felting may be necessary to remove any signs of the addition of fiber.

Using a deep mold to felt dimensional objects:

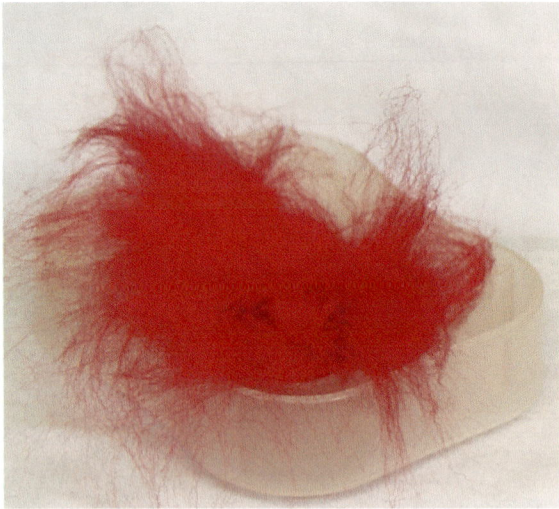

A deep mold can be used to create dimensional objects and can be particularly useful when you want objects of identical size.

For these objects the mold or cookie cutter must be stuffed very full of fiber.

Felt the fiber paying particular care when felting around the edges of the mold.

Turn the mold over and felt from the other side as well.

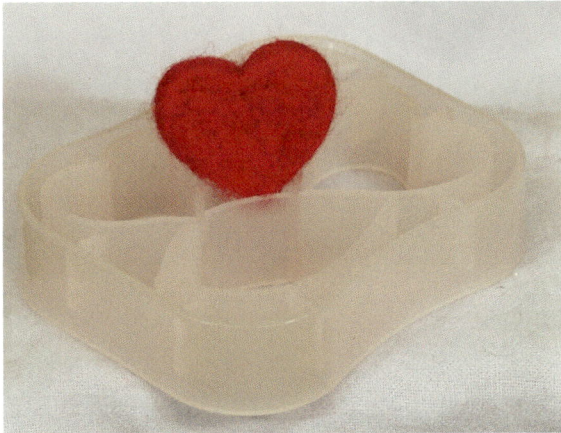

Remove the object from the mold and felt around the edges.

If you desire, you can round the flat edges caused by the mold.

Additional needling will reduce the size and increase the firmness of the object.

This could be a very nice bead!

If you intend to make multiple objects of the same size using this method, be sure that you stuff the mold equally for each individual piece.

What do you do if you didn't have enough fiber in your deep mold?

The best way to add more fiber to a deep felted object that has already received quite a bit of felting is to remove it from the mold, then add new fiber to the mold and place the object in the *middle* (shown in blue), then fold the added fibers over the top and resume felting.

It is even better if you use carded fiber for this rather than drummed fiber as shown in this photo. This will prevent the appearance of LAYERS on your deep mold felted object.

Chapter Eight: Creating Flat Shapes

Carded versus Drummed Fiber:

In the majority of the flat felt examples shown, I have used drummed or aligned fiber with the exception of the freeform flat felted object. Why? Is using drummed fiber a superior method? No, it certainly is not. We've seen how core fiber is easier to felt because it is not drummed and the same holds true for any other fiber. Carding is the easiest way to break the drummed alignment of the fibers.

So why ever use drummed fiber without carding it first?

Drummed fiber can be easier to measure which is important when trying to make matching pieces. It is easier to control the thickness when using drummed fiber.

Carding fiber will make felting easier and will allow you to blend colors.

With experience you will learn when you should take the time to card the fiber and when you do not need to. You may find that you always prefer to card your fiber or that you avoid it at all costs. Whatever works best for you!

Carpe Diem

Blending Fibers with carding brushes:

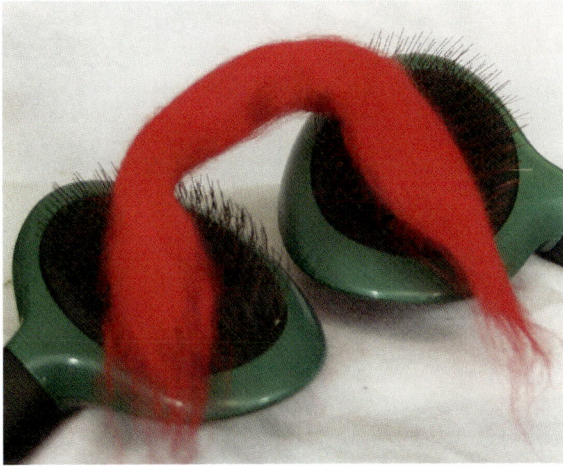

Pictured are two wire dog brushes and some fiber.
Wire dog brushes are generally cheaper than carding brushes and work well for needle felters.

Tear the long fiber into lengths of about 2 or 3 inches long.
How much fiber you can blend at a time will depend on the size of your brushes. It is generally easier to have less than too much.

Tear 2" to 3" lengths from the fiber you wish to blend into the original color and lay that on top.

With the handles pointing away from one another begin to brush the fibers.

Do this a lot!

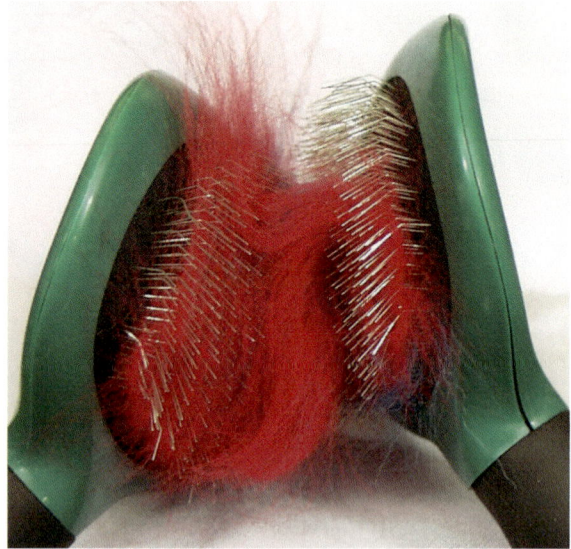

Now and then you want to remove the fiber you have been brushing from the wire. Do this by holding both handles in the same direction and let one brush pull the fiber off the other

Oh dear! It hasn't blended very well yet!

Turn the handles away from one another and brush some more!

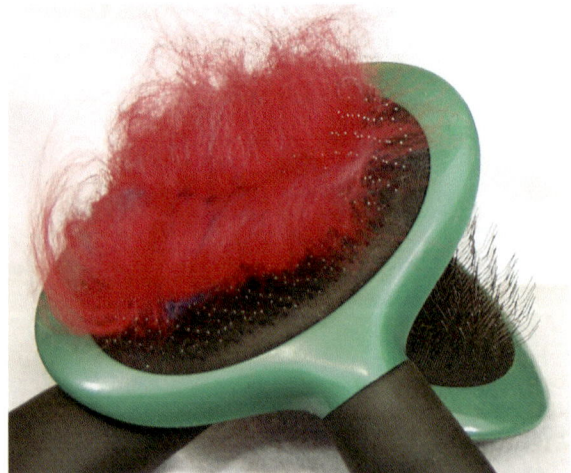

This is the basic process – handles away from one another blends. Handles in the same direction removes the fiber from the wires.

Repeat until the two colors are nicely blended.
Now remove some of that blended fiber and put it aside. (1)

Add some more of the contrast fiber.

Repeat the process of brushing until the new combination is well blended together.
Take some of that fiber away and set it aside. (2)

Now add some more blue fiber.

Chapter Nine: Blending and Decorating

Brush, remove, and brush again until it is all well blended.

Take away some of the fiber, set it aside (3) and add some more blue.

Brush and remove and brush and remove until it is all blended together. (4)

And here you have the results – a very nice gradation from red to blue.

From left to right: (1) (2) (3) (4)

You could make even more "steps" then the four color blends produced here.

You can blend more than two colors together at a time.

You can simply card one color fiber to break the alignment of drummed fiber.

As long as you remember which colors you blended and their approximate proportions it is easy to blend more if you didn't blend enough.

Making "yarn":

No, I'm not going to teach you how to spin yarn. I use the term "yarn" because that most closely resembles the finished product but this "yarn" has certain characteristics that are useful for felting.

From a length of fiber, gently separate enough strands to be a bit thicker than you want your finished "yarn" to be.

The ends tend to be wispy and not as full as the fiber in the middle, so fold the end back on itself.

Using a tool or a pin, secure one end to your work surface and, using your fingers, twist the length of fiber.

Using your needle or needle tool, felt along the length of the twisted fiber.

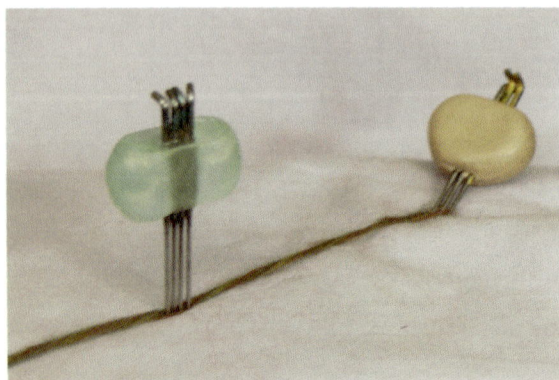

When you have felted the full length of your fiber, gently lift it, twist it again and felt along the length again.

Remember to fold back the wispy bits at the non-secured end and felt them into the "yarn" as well.

You've just created a piece of "yarn" which is useful for decorating, for outlining eyes and many other purposes.

How thick your "yarn" is depends on how much fiber you used.

The most important thing to note about this "yarn" is that all the fibers have NOT been felted in to make it smooth. Those loose fibers will help to felt it into other objects.

Let's put some on a ball.

Use your needle to anchor the end in place.

Needle it in place as you arrange it on your object.

I find that my "three together" tool with #42 needles works very well for this process.

Chapter Nine: Blending and Decorating

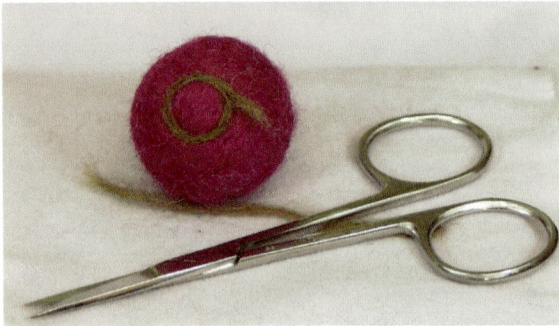

Want to close the circle? Cut the excess fiber off at an angle. This will make it easier to conceal where the "yarn" ended.

Felt it well!

A very nice circle.

This is an easy method to decorate a surface.

Such decoration could be done without first creating "yarn" but it provides you with easier control of the width of the decorative fiber.

Painting with fiber:

Here is a sphere being embellished with silk fiber.

The technique is almost identical to that of embellishing with "yarn" except that the fibers being applied are loose. You control the amount of fiber actually being felted as you go.

This allows subtle changes in color and width as the silk fibers are felted to the sphere.

It is just a matter of controlling the amount of fiber being felted.

You can make your design have both thin and wide sections.

As you can see, silk fiber looks lovely felted over wool.

Any fiber can be used to "paint" the surface of your object. Needle at a shallow angle to the object and allow the barbs to pull the fiber into place.

I've used an old Pritten head in this and the next few photos.

You can paint a very fine line without a great deal of effort.

Excess "painting" fiber is simply trimmed with scissors.

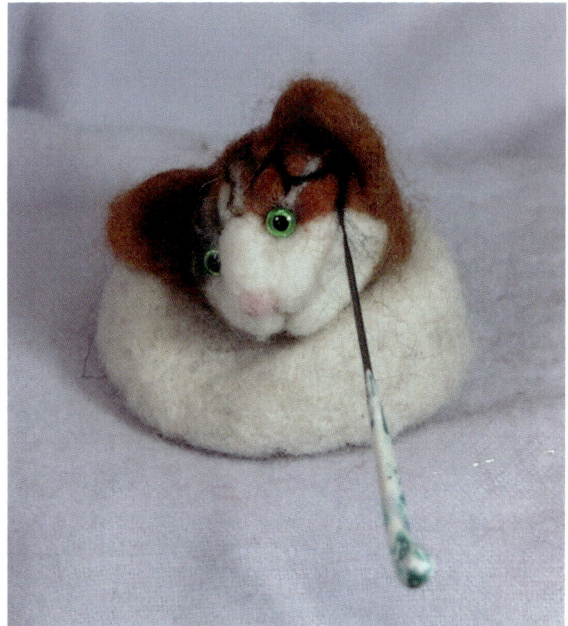

You can felt in one color and felt over that with another color if you wish.

The quantity of fiber being used to "paint" is so minimal that there is no significant increase in size to the object being "painted".

Do zigzags or any pattern that suits your fancy.

Painting with fiber is just very controlled surface felting.

It allows you a lot of creative possibilities while being frugal with your dress fiber.

Once felted into your object your "painted" fiber should be even/level with the surrounding areas. There should be no distortion to the surface that indicates that the "painted" fiber was applied at a later time than the surrounding surface.

By lightly surface felting both the painted fiber and surrounding areas can assist in making the "painted" embellishments one with the whole.

Combining Simple Shapes to make Complex Shapes:

What are the simple shapes?

Flat shapes: Square, circle, triangle, rectangle, oval etc.

Three Dimensional shapes: Cube/box, sphere, cone, cylinder, etc.

These are the basic building blocks of any object.

Want to make a cupcake? That's just a truncated cone topped with a half-sphere.
Want to make a dog? You'll need a big fat cylinder for the body, narrower cylinders for the legs, an egg or a cone enhanced sphere for the head and flat triangles or truncated flat ovals for the ears.

Building Blocks Flat and Three Dimensional:

You should now know how to make both flat and three dimensional objects. You understand that sometimes it is worth while to make one form out of two parts so that you can control the firmness of each part.

Once you begin to see more complex objects as a combination of simple shapes you can make just about anything. The problems you will face in making these more complex objects are not as much in how to construct them, but more about maintaining proper proportion.

Peking Tom

Armatures:

An armature is a supportive core, often made of wire, which is used to hold up a sculpture.

Some needle felters swear by armatures. They believe that they give strength to a finished sculpture and allow the figure to be posed. Armatures can be difficult to work around, have the potential to rust (unless you take the necessary precautions of using only non-rusting wire) and the potential to break. The figure cannot be as firmly felted not only because of the difficulty felting firmly around an armature but also because there needs to be some flexibility so the figure can be posed. They encourage handling of the figure which will increase the wear and tear on the figure. I have made figures with armatures and I have made far more figures without armatures. An armature is not needed for strength. Good firm felting will provide the necessary strength. So the choice to use or not use an armature becomes a personal and artistic call.

There are many types of armatures. In needle felting wire armatures are most common and they can be very complex or very simple.

Let's make a very simple armature. Here are two pieces of wire of roughly the same length.

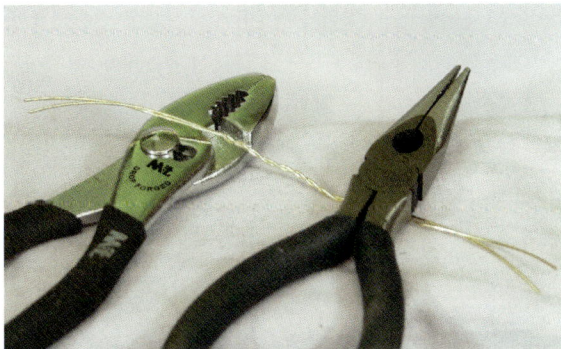

Use two pairs of pliers, one to hold the two pieces of wire and the other to twist the wire.

The ends, which were not twisted, have been folded downward and separated.

Perhaps it is the framework for a swing set.

Perhaps it is the legs and body of an animal.

It probably isn't a good idea to just leave the ends like that. Using needle nose pliers the tips can be curled back to form a loop and eliminate the possibility of the sharp end poking through the fiber.

Sometimes a partial armature is a useful and even necessary addition to a piece. I'll demonstrate that later.

Making things:

Let's start out with something very simple: a pear. The closest of the simple shapes discussed earlier would be an egg, which is almost pear shaped.

You could simply make a pear shape with the core fiber, but transforming an egg into a pear shape is a matter of needling the smaller end further down towards the larger end.

Another option would have been to make a sphere and add a cone, but this is not necessary. You will not be doing any fancy sculpting on the top end of the pear that would require anything more than a nicely felted, medium firm egg or pear shape.

From here it is a simple process of dressing the pear shape with pear colored fibers, which you would felt securely to the core.

A thin cylinder added to the top makes a stem.

A bit of darker fiber is needled into the bottom and your pear is complete.

How about an artichoke?

Basically the form of an artichoke is that of an egg for the body with a cylinder for the stem. Add some leaves to that and you've got an artichoke.

You may note that I have flared one end of the cylinder. This is to mimic where the stem projects from the globe of the artichoke.

Here the stem has been covered and both deep and surface felted. The fiber has been left un-felted at the flared end of the cylinder. This will provide fibers to felt the cylinder/stem to the globe.

Using the triangle flat felting technique, the basic triangle was felted and the bottom, loose fibers were folded up and felted to form a rounded bottom leaf shape.

This leaf shape was felted very firmly.

Trying the leaf on for size:

It would take three leaves of this size to surround the tip of the egg/globe. It will take many more leaves to cover the complete globe.

It is better to stop and check your proportions prior to mass producing a number of similar items only to find out that they are out of scale.

Many more leaves have been felted and have been pinned in place over the foundation egg/globe.

Pinning parts into place as you're working is a very good means of checking the progress of the project. Does it look the way it should? Are there any obvious errors in proportions? Is there something I should correct now which will be difficult to correct after the piece is felted together?

It is looking more and more like an artichoke. Now we can start to actually felt the leaves into place.

Chapter Ten: Combining Simple Shapes and Forms

Unlike when the leaves were pinned into place it is possible to felt the first three leaves to almost conform to the curve of the egg/globe foundation below.

This provides a realistic detail.

The leaves are felted into place around the egg/globe and the stem is felted to the bottom of the globe.

That's a nice artichoke!

Perhaps you can see how this approach to making an artichoke might be modified to make a flower.

Let's try a project that is a bit more complex and at the same time relatively simple. I've chosen a subject which will require several different basic shapes to make the whole but because of the intended purpose of this project, it does not need to be super firmly felted. It will introduce a bit of sculpting, the use of thread (or embroidery floss), adding eyes and the use of a specialty fiber to great effect.

Let's make a sheep pin cushion. Because this object is to be a pin cushion it will not need to be super firmly felted and detailed.

The basic body shape resembles half an egg (our sheep is laying down on the ground - a good position for a pin cushion)

The head of the sheep is rather pear shaped. You could start with a log and add fiber on one end or just aim to make a small pear. Use whichever method you prefer.

Dress the head with better fiber if you don't like the look of the core fiber.

The dressing fiber does not need to be well surface felted into place. It needs to just be felted enough to secure it.

We will be doing more work on the head later.

Chapter Ten: Combining Simple Shapes and Forms

Dress the body with brown fiber – unless your sheep has a white fleece and a black head.

Your sheep can be any color or combination of colors that you prefer.

Make a thin cylinder a little wider than the front end of your sheep and dress it with fiber. This is going to act as the front legs folded under.

Felt the cylinder into place.

Make two short cylinders the same thickness as the front leg cylinder and dress them with fiber. These will be the hind legs of the sheep (well as much of the leg as we need to show).

Notice that I added a bit of the brown fiber under where the head will be positioned and over the central section of the long thin cylinder for the front legs. This forms the chest, and makes it appear that the sheep has its front hooves tucked under.

Chapter Ten: Combining Simple Shapes and Forms

Make two truncated ovals from the dress fiber for the ears. Some sheep have rather pointed ears, some do not. Some ears are erect and others flop over.

Pin them in place to see how it is looking!

Any of these pieces parts could be rendered in great detail if you wanted to take the time. It would be possible to felt what look like hooves, but that would require more fiber and firmer felting.

Several changes have been made to the head. The sides of the muzzle were more firmly felted to assist with shaping a nose. A mouth was also defined. Thread was used to further define the nose, muzzle and mouth and also to secure two large black beads to serve as eyes.

The head and ears were also felted to the body, which I shaped further.

Brown curly Romney fiber was used for this sheep's fleece. The fiber was positioned and felted into any of the areas that previously were brown and also extended to the top of the sheep's head.

The ears were felted a little further in to shorten their length, and the Romney fleece was felted to hint at hips, knees, and elbows.

Not baaaa-d!!

Chapter Ten: Combining Simple Shapes and Forms

Time to try something even more complex: This project requires many pieces and will include the use of partial armatures. While the completed object is complex, all the parts are made from simple shapes:

Let's make a Dalek. If you are not familiar with Doctor Who you will probably have no idea what a Dalek is. Basically it is rather like a robot without traditional legs and arms.

We start off with a truncated cone of medium firm density. This one is about 3" high. I've flattened the normally curved surface to form a total of 10 facets.

I intend to dress the cone with this grey fiber but first I have made 3 grey flat circles that are about the same diameter as the top of the cone. I've also made three smaller and thicker black circles that will act as spacers for the grey circles.

In addition I have also made a half sphere in grey.

I made the half sphere using the round mold and concentrating most of the fiber in the center. Once removed from the mold, I further refined the half sphere shape.

While it isn't absolutely necessary to dress the facets of the cone individually, doing so helps to reinforce and increase their definition. I used drummed fiber and began surface felting at the top, working my way down the side of the facet until it was tacked into place.

I then turned the cone over and repeated surface felting.

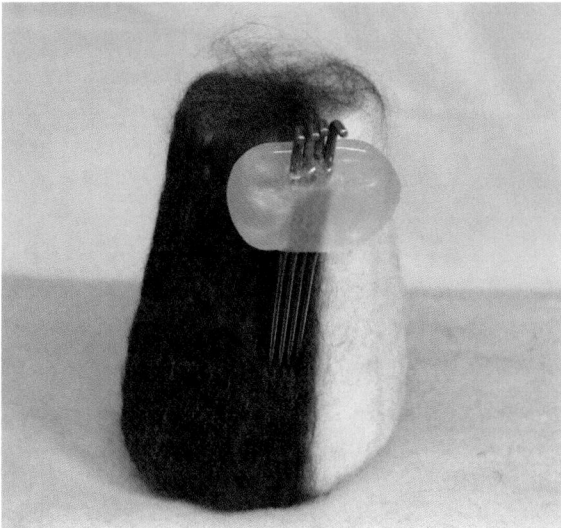

Repeat this process until all facets have been securely surface felted.

When all the facets have been felted, felt the fluffy ends into the top and bottom of the truncated cone.

Now lets pin the "head" into place following this order (as seen)

Half sphere
Black flat circle
Grey flat circle
Black flat circle
Grey flat circle
Black flat circle
Grey flat circle
Truncated cone

Daleks have a bumper around the bottom and although theirs is faceted as are their sides, for demonstration purposes we'll just do a simple bumper.

This bumper could be made up either as a very thick "yarn," by making a long thin cylinder or by using the basic technique for making a long oval.

There are many ways to reach the same ends.

Chapter Ten: Combining Simple Shapes and Forms

For the next step, I have created two long flat rectangles. They are each long enough to circle the truncated cone just under the "head" which is where they will be placed.

Pin them in place to get an idea of how it is coming along.

That looked pretty good so I've felted all the pieces together, starting with the grey circle placed on top of the truncated cone and finishing with the half sphere.

The long rectangular pieces were felted into place as well.

I cut a piece of wire about 2" long, and used needle nose pliers to curl the end that will be outside the object. This partial armature is wrapped with white fiber and carefully felted up and down the length of the wire as seen in the photo at the left.

After carefully felting the white fiber, black fiber has been added to the curled wire end and felted into a cone shape.

This armature represents the "eye" of the Dalek.

Two small cross hatched slits made with the Exacto knife assist inserting the "eye" into the half sphere of the head.

The loose fibers that were left at the end of the armature are felted well into the half sphere.

A tiny cylinder was made in white fiber and felted to the half sphere as shown.

I'm not really certain what purpose this cylinder has for the Dalek. I tend to think of it as a snorkel.

Two more partial armatures have been created, wrapped and felted with fiber and inserted below the eye at the front of the Dalek. These are weapons of some nature. I believe in the original Doctor Who series one of these parts was made from a toilet plunger!

A long flat rectangle was made out of black fiber. It needed to be very well felted because it is cut into sections and felted into place as seen in the photo on the left.

A lot of small spheres were made by pulling off a small portion of carded black fiber and rolling it in between palms. These were not very firm at all. Since the desired end result is to have half spheres adorning the bottom facets of the Dalek, firmness of the small spheres was not critical.

When you begin to view your project ideas in terms of simple shapes and forms, you break it into manageable parts. None of the simple parts that were used in the making of the previous examples were significantly manipulated, but manipulation of parts greatly expands the possibilities.

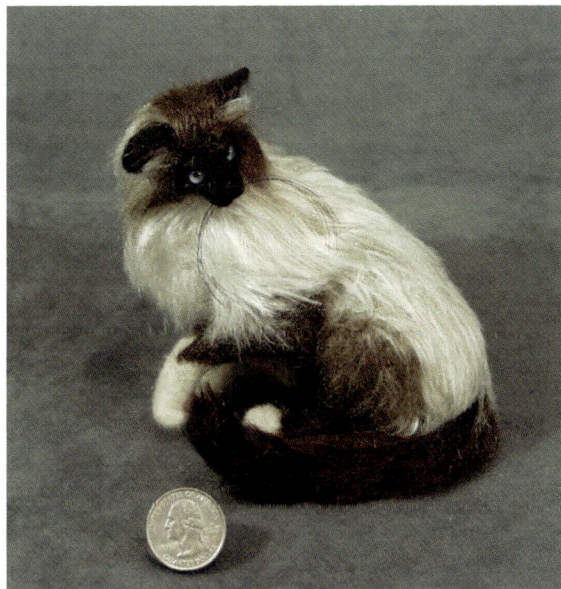

Victoria

Chapter Ten: Combining Simple Shapes and Forms

Constructing open and hollow objects:

Not all needle felted projects result in solid objects. Sometimes you may want to make an object that is open or even hollow. Such objects need to be firmly felted to support their own structure or will require an armature (partial or whole) for support.

Let's make a cart. We'll need a good bottom for the cart that will maintain its shape.
Here core fiber has been laid out in a basic rectangle.

The majority of the needling has been done on the top and bottom of the rectangle, with only a minor bit of needling done on the sides and ends to refine the shape to medium firmness.

Medium firmness of the core fiber is strong enough to act as a good bottom for our cart.

The bottom has been dressed with red fiber which has been surface felted into place.

This additional felting increases the strength of our bottom.

Sides for the cart could be made either as four separate pieces or in one long piece.
It may be easier to control the width of the sides doing it in one long piece.
It is also possible at this point to cut the long piece into the side sections which would then require joining of corners to construct the cart.
I've opted for just using the one long piece and using needling to define corners.

Core fiber longer than the perimeter of the cart was laid out, lightly felted and then folded over on itself and felted again. This results in one smooth edge and one feathered edge.

Red fiber has been folded over the smooth edge of the core fiber and both surface and deep felted. As expected, core fiber can be seen in the dressed fiber surface.
The sides will be redressed later to hide this core fiber.

Here, as with just the core fiber previously, you have a smooth edge and a feathered edge.

The long side piece has been pinned in place to the rectangular bottom of the cart.

The feathered edge of the side extends below where the sides and the bottom will be joined. The excess will be folded over the bottom and needled into place.

Perhaps you can anticipate what possible problem is about to arise.

Chapter Eleven: Creating Hollow Objects

Here the sides have been joined to the bottom. The excess length of the side piece was trimmed and the sections joined. When carefully done, the result is an invisible seam.

While the core fiber does add strength, it is not sufficient to make needling the excess feathered edge of the sides to the bottom easy.

The solution is to cut a piece of packing foam to fit inside the open bed of the cart.

Here the cart in progress is pictured sitting upon that foam support.

Placing the foam inside the cart bed and turning the whole over allows you to securely surface felt the feathered edge to the bottom.

Packing foam is very useful for supports of this nature. It is easy to cut to the needed size and resists the needles which prevent actually felting anything to the foam support.

The sides have been felted to the bottom and the excess feathered edge of the sides and been folded over and surface felted into place.

The corners are obviously a bit rounded at this point and the upper edge of the cart is a bit irregular. The irregularity could have been avoided by creating the piece for the sides more carefully but it is useful to know what you can do when a flaw such as this happens in the making of an object.

Chapter Eleven: Creating Hollow Objects

There are several options to resolve the irregularity of the top edge of the sides. One would be to carefully trim and redress the edge; another is to disguise the problem with the addition of another decorative element.

Here I've added some fat "yarn" to the top edge of the sides. The foam support was put back into place to make the process of felting the "yarn" to the sides easier.

It's time to redress the sides of the cart which still showed some exposed core fiber.

I've used drummed fiber the width of the sides and carefully surface felted it in place, working one side at a time. The foam support makes this task easier.

This wouldn't be much of a cart if it didn't have wheels.

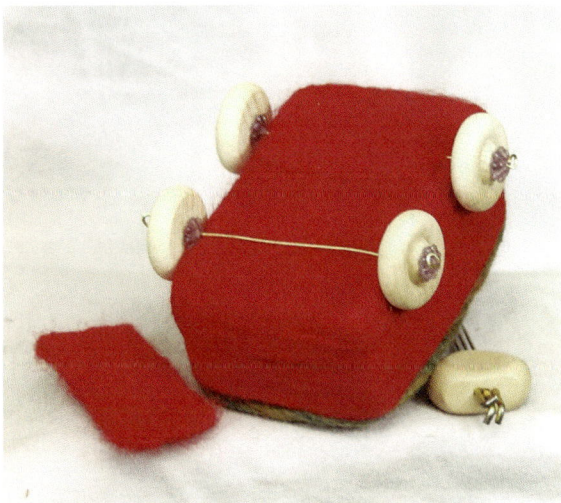

It would be possible to make felt wheels by using a round mold and deep felting four matching pieces. I've used wooden wheels and a bit of wire to act as an axle.

Note also that I have created a flat rectangle that is as wide as the cart and obviously wider than the wire axle.

With the foam support in place, the rectangle is surface felted to the bottom to both hide and secure the axle.

There it is: a completed cart and the wheels actually turn.

The corners here were left rounded but could have been defined by careful needling.

Additional designs could have been surface felted to the sides. The wheels could have been painted. A handle to pull the cart could have been added.

The use of a temporary foam support makes such projects possible or, at the very least, easier.

The cart was an open object which isn't exactly the same as hollow. So let's see how that might be done.

First we need something to occupy the space that we wish to remain empty. Here I've chosen a wooden egg.

Wood works well for this purpose but so does Styrofoam. A wooden form can be used repeatedly whereas the Styrofoam may end up being destroyed in the process.

The wooden egg was wrapped twice around with core fiber, removing excess fiber where necessary and surface felted to a great degree. This is no easy task and is time consuming. Always be careful to angle your needles so that they will not hit and break upon the wooden egg.

You want to try to keep the thickness of the fiber as uniform as possible.

Chapter Eleven: Creating Hollow Objects

I've chosen to surface dress this egg in a carded and blended brown color.

I surface felt the dressing fiber very well into the core fiber beneath. This increases the firmness of the core fiber.

Always be aware of that hard wooden egg in the center to avoid breaking needles.

When the egg is firmly felted, I use an Exacto knife and cut the felted egg off of the wooden egg.

Such a cut needs to be placed so that the solid form can be removed. If this had been cut closer to the tip of the egg it would be impossible to remove the wooden egg.

Be careful to cut all the way through to the underlying support or you will find some fibers uncut that will pull on your felted egg shell as you attempt to remove it.

Eggstraordinary!

Creating a hollow object over a solid form that can be used again and again is useful but sometimes you may wish to create a hollow form for which you have no wooden support. Styrofoam can be used as an inner support and it can be cut to desired shape.

While you do not need to be afraid of sticking your needles into the Styrofoam you should avoid doing so frequently. Ultimately the fiber and Styrofoam can be separated from one another but any fibers that have been poked deeply into the Styrofoam will tend to pull when the foam foundation is removed.

It is completely possible to just needle felt the fiber around your support but you may wish to consider wet felting the foundation fiber into place after initial needle felting. It is an extremely long and awkward process to just needle felt the fiber into place. Wet felting is easier for such a project. You must wait for a wet felted object to be completely dry before you do any additional needle felting. Moisture can cause your needles to rust.

Wet Felting:

I'm not going to go into much detail on this subject, but I will cover the basics. I think it is best to start with a core fiber. Batting, as I have previously described, lends itself well to this purpose. To start I cover my object with a layer of the core fiber (batting) and needle felt it securely into place.

Fill a sink with hot soapy water. Submerge the item to be felted into the water and using bubble wrap with the small bubbles or just your fingers, agitate the fiber around your form. Try to agitate all areas equally.

It will all seem like a large sloppy mess and you'll be convinced that it is never going to felt, but it will. It just takes some time. When the fibers do begin to felt try to maintain a uniform thickness. Once it is felted nicely set it somewhere to dry completely.

Once they are dry, you can needle felt on wet felted objects.

Let's make a squash.

Starting out with a 4" diameter Styrofoam ball, I cut off a small section to make a flat bottom.

I covered the flat bottom with core fiber (batting) slightly larger than the bottom. I wrap the rest of the sphere with core fiber removing excess fiber to conform to the sphere shape. I then needle all the fiber securely together.

It was wet felted and left to dry.

To make ribs on the squash take some core fiber that measures almost the height from top to cut bottom.

There are a couple of obvious ways to join this fiber to the foundation. You can just needle felt it on the foundation sphere and spend a lot of time contouring it to form a nice rib or ....

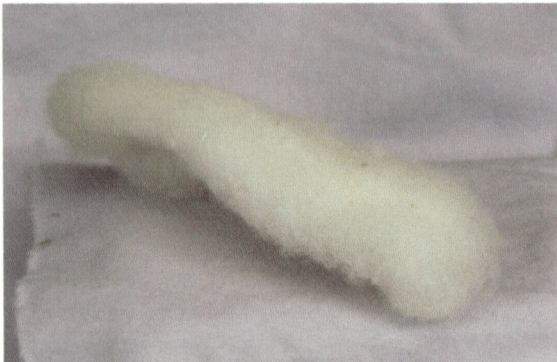

You could do a lot of that needle felting before you add the rib to the sphere.

The second approach is actually easier and faster because you can needle more effectively on your work surface than you can on a sphere where you are trying to avoid piercing the Styrofoam.

For a rib you want the center to be thicker and the edges feathered.

With a lot of surface needling, the rib was secured to the foundation sphere and additional ribs created and added.

Continue this process until you have the sphere completely covered with these ribs, and then surface felt generously.

If you needed to you could add additional fiber to fatten up a rib.

The ribs should be at very least medium firm at this point.

It's really best to aim for the finished project to be very firm. This will provide strength and decrease the possibility of distortion when it comes time to cut a top later.

Cover it all with your dressing fiber and surface felt until your hands ache and you wonder why in the world you ever took up needle felting.

Create a stem as you would make a thin cylinder. Keep the end that will be felted into the squash less firmly felted, but really firmly felting the upper portion will allow you to create the ridges that exist on the stems for real pumpkins and squash.

Felt the stem to the top of the squash. If it doesn't seem to felt down as well as you like, add a bit of extra fiber to assist.

Using an Exacto knife, cut around the squash to form a top.

This all looks good so far but there is actually a tactical error in the planning of this squash box which I will discuss in some detail a picture or two from now.

Using a rounded tip palette knife, carefully begin to cut the Styrofoam ball out.

A round tipped palette knife will cut Styrofoam easily but will not cut your fibers!

I find that it is easiest to get the center section out first and then carefully slice out the rest.

Yes, there will be Styrofoam piffle as a result. You can try gently brushing it off or using some tape to lift it off.

So there you have it, a squash box.

When you make an object such as this, it is handy to create an obvious orientation marker for properly aligning top and bottom. In the following photo you'll see that I added a bit of a green stripe to act as this orientation marker.

It looks pretty nice but there is a basic problem. When the top is set in place some of that white core fiber is certain to show.

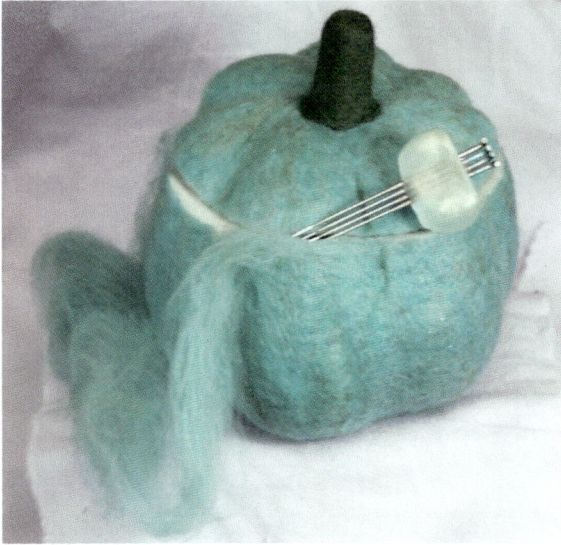

One solution would be to carefully felt some fiber to cover the outside edge of the core.

That would certainly work, but there were other options that might have been used prior to cutting the top off.

Core fiber was used to provide strength.

Wet felting was used because it was the easiest method to tightly felt the foundation around the Styrofoam foundation.

Core fiber was used to create the ribs partially for strength, partially because it is more economical and partially for ease of felting.

What construction alternatives could have been included to avoid the problem of some of the white core showing when the top is set into place?

A much thicker layer of dress fiber could have been applied.

Dying the core fiber is an option, but that gets into learning how to dye wool and deciding if you dye it before you begin to apply it to the Styrofoam ball or after.

Another option is to use some other decorative means of obscuring the white area: beads, sequins, embroidery floss, or bias tape. There is no law that the top has to sit directly on the bottom so any number of decorative fillers could be put into place.

Felting around an object:

This is identical to creating a hollow object except that you do not remove the object around which you have felted. You might want to felt around an object in order to add weight to a piece such as a paper weight, or you might want to cover a jingle bell to make an ornament or a cat toy.

When you do felt around an object always be careful with your needles.

Taffy

Other techniques:

Sooner or later you are bound to want to make a creature that has eyes. Eyes are available in many sizes and qualities. Some come with a post making it easy to insert into your project and other eyes have no post.

Here are some eyes without posts that I got from Van Dyke's Taxidermy. They do sell these same eyes with posts but I find it cheaper to just add my own.

First, I made a polymer clay rest for the eyes. Since I almost always used the same size eyes, this one rest works for all my purposes.

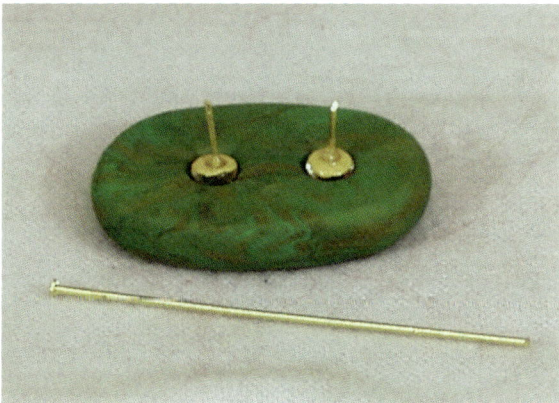

Here you can see two eyes to which posts have been added.

In the foreground is the jewelry finding I use to create posts. These findings are available in most craft stores.

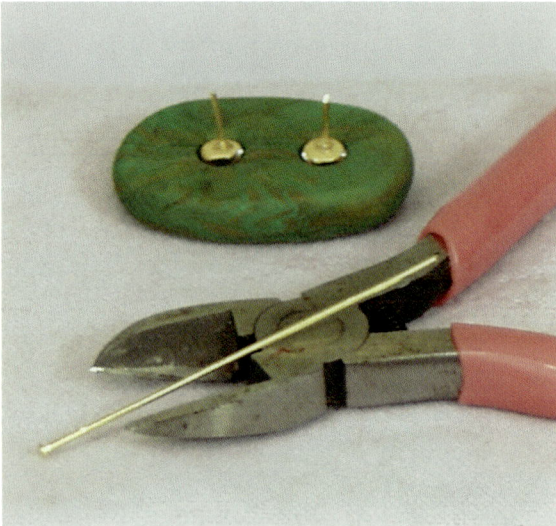

Using wire cutters I snip the finding at an angle about ½ inch from the head of the finding.

The post should be long enough to insert into the head of whatever you are making but not so long that there is any chance of it sticking out the other side.

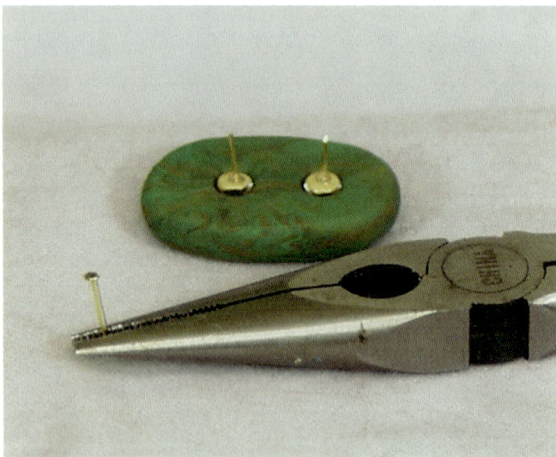

Using needle nose pliers, dip the head into a good quality glue (such as E6000 or Gorilla Glue) and then position the post in the center of the back of the eye.

Let this dry completely.

Your eyes are now ready for use.

If you purchase eyes that have posts you may find it helpful to cut the posts at a sharp angle. This will make it easier to insert the eye into your form.

It is quite possible to needle felt eyes.

Adding fiber is a simple process. You grab a bit of fiber and you needle it in – no big deal. Let's take a look at adding some fiber for a very specific purpose and learn a few other things along the way.

Looks like it is time for this fruit to take on some PEARsonality!

Let's gather up some fiber for a nose. Note that the loose fiber in this photo is roughly arranged in the shape of a nose and is HUGE compared to the pear. Felting those fibers will considerably reduce their size!

Do keep in mind that you want more fiber in the tip and bridge of the nose than you do elsewhere. So as you needle direct more fiber to the area of most need.

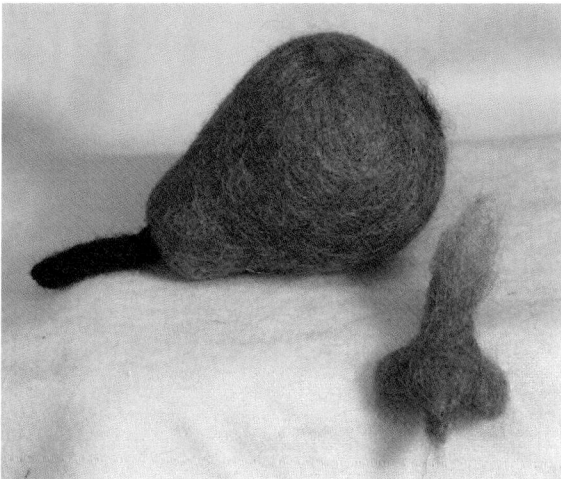

It's easier to felt the fibers for the nose on the work surface than on the pear since so much reduction and refinement is needed.

It should still appear too large when it is finally time to attach it to the pear.

It is important to keep in mind the purpose of the object you are creating. This pear will be ornamental and not receive much handling. If he were going to be handled frequently, everything should be more firmly felted.

I personally like to first attach the tip of the bridge and the portion just above the lips (if there were lips) before I start felting the nose into place.

The process is one of surface felting combined with some gentle deep felting.

Sometimes it will be necessary to rest the side or tip of the nose on the work surface to be able to felt the main section of the nose more firmly.

He needs eyes!

These have been temporarily inserted to check for placement.

Once satisfied with the placement, I use my two-needle tool (a single #38 needle will work fine too) to establish some needle holes around where the eye was placed.

You should be able to see those holes where the right eye (our right, not the Pear's right) has been removed.

Now why do that? Since I want these eyes to be recessed into the pear head, I created these guide holes tell me where the eye will be placed.

If I started needling fiercely to recess that area, the surrounding fiber would also be pulled into that depression distorting the face. What to do?

Use your Exacto knife to carefully cut the fibers following the needle hole guide line.

I call this Controlled Cutting. It should only be done where fibers have been sufficiently surface felted and when you do not want surrounding fiber pulled by further needling.

In the photo here I've needled two good depressions into which the eyes will be set. The depressions may seem smaller than the eyes but remember, fiber (unless super firm) will give.

Here are the eyes set into those depressions – note that the surrounding area of the pear has not been distorted.

If pleased with the results, now would be the time to glue the eyes into place. You could either completely remove the eye and apply a bit of glue on the back, or you could half remove the eye and carefully apply some glue with a tooth pick or a piece of wire. It doesn't take a lot of glue.

Let the glue dry completely before you make any other details to the eyes.

He needs a mouth!

This mouth was created by needling a line. I've decided to not devote much effort to his upper lip, but I do want him to have a pouty lower lip so I've taken a bit of fiber and made a crude cylinder.

The lower lip is felted into place in much the same way as the nose. It's all a matter of surface and deep felting while refining the shape of the available fiber.

To further define the mouth I took just a very few dark brown fibers and needled those into the line that formed the mouth.

Had I wanted to, I could have taken my Exacto knife and cut the length of the mouth and actually opened the mouth up. It would have been necessary to dress felt the exposed interior but that would not have been difficult.

Here a leaf has been added to be hair or a hat.

The leaf was both surface and deep felted to the pear head approximately along the central vein of the leaf. The front edge was curled back and gently felted to maintain the shape.

I've added some very loosely felted fiber to form eyebrows. They could be pulled off without a great deal of effort but this pear is not destined to be submitted to such rough treatment.

A truncated oval with the feathered ends felted well into the mouth makes a tongue.

I've also blended some fibers to add some blush to his cheeks and surface felted that into place.

Chapter Twelve: More Advanced Techniques

More manipulation, sculpting and other useful things:

Let's make a dragon!

Here I have a firm sphere dressed in purple fiber to which I added a medium firm cone made of the same purple fiber.

I do not intend to manipulate the sphere portion much at all but do intend to sculpt a dragon face.

The firmer your object becomes, the more defined your sculpting can be, but you need to start defining during the medium firm stage and gradually refine it as you continue.

Here you can see that I have sculpted an elongated diamond shape down the forehead of the dragon.

I've also started to establish the location of the eyes by making depressions where they will go.

I will use controlled cutting to recess the eyes without distorting the surrounding area.

I've sculpted a mouth and used some controlled cutting to free that over hanging upper lip from the lower lip. The mouth was further defined by the addition of dark fiber.

The eyes have been recessed at an angle so that they look forward. Eyelids were created and felted into place.

The elongated diamond depression on the forehead has been filled and felted with the contrasting fiber.

This is another perspective of the same head.

In this photo, it is easier to see the additional sculpting that defines the nose ridges.

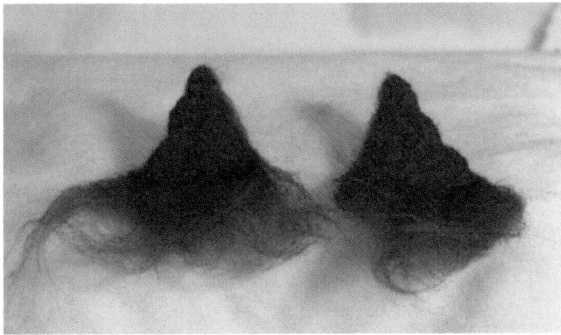

Ears: These were made in much the same manner as the flat felted triangle, but I've pulled in the edge on one side to create a ripple effect.

There was a lot of excess fiber in those ears so I've cut it off. You may note that the cut is curved and that one side is shorter than the other. The ears have been cut in this manner so that they will fit on the spherical head with the tips pointing more upright.

If I wanted the ears to point straight up I would have had to shorten that side even more.

Here are the ears on the head. Learning how to attach ears is mostly a matter of experience.

Since the ears were cut to conform to the shape of the head, there were not any long fibers to deeply felt into the head.

You can add some long fibers to the ears prior to attachment. When it comes time to attach the head to the body, additional fiber will be added, which can be used to reinforce the ears.

I've made a body out of core fiber and pinned the head in place.

This looks like it will be about right but should I need to make adjustments to the body there is still plenty of opportunity to do so.

Here is another angle of the head pinned to the body. The body actually looks a bit too short; some curvature to the neck would also be an improvement.

Adding fiber to the body at this point is very easy, and since the body is only medium firm, many manipulations (such as increasing the curve to the under belly) are still possible.

When your object is medium firm you can use your hands to twist, curve and change the shape, then needle to hold the changes you have made.

Legs were created on doll needles with core fiber. Doll needles are ideal for this purpose because they are long, rigid and thin.

Core fiber tends to add strength, ease of felting and saves money by not using up your more expensive dress fiber.

Chapter Twelve: More Advanced Techniques

Here are two of the legs covered with dressed fiber. These have been both surface and deep felted, which has caused some of the core fiber to be revealed. No worries!

These legs are going to go through a lot more before the dragon is done and they will end up being redressed with fiber to regain some of the dimension which will be lost during the felting process.

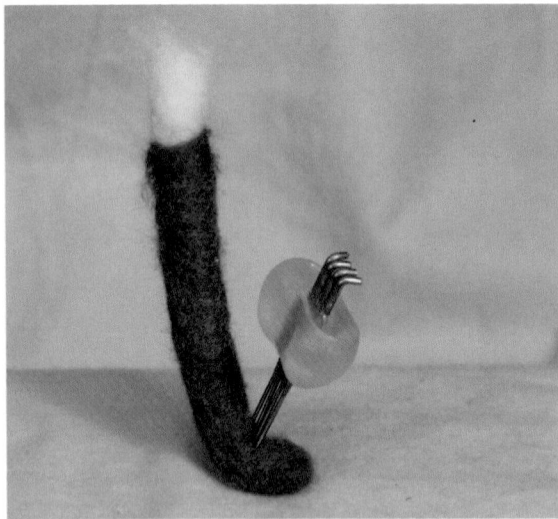

I have removed the doll needle so the leg is easy to manipulate.

To create a foot, bend the cylinder near the end and needle well to help establish that change.

You could make the foot separately and attach it to the cylinder/leg. You could make all the parts for a leg (foot, shin, and thigh) separately if you preferred, but I find that it is easier to control the length and uniformity of legs by manipulating thin cylinders.

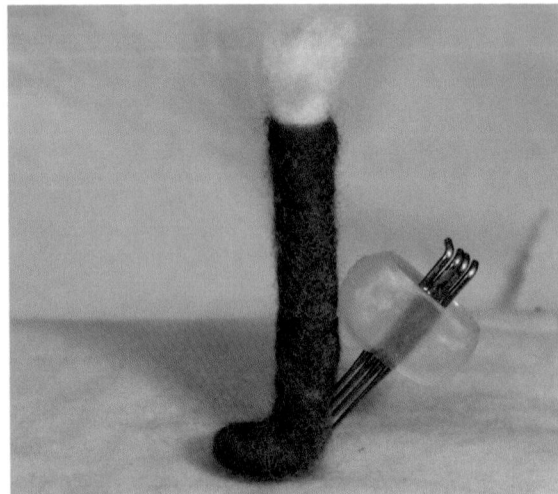

Needle that angle bend from the other side too. In fact, needle it from every possible direction, front, sides and back to set the bend in place.

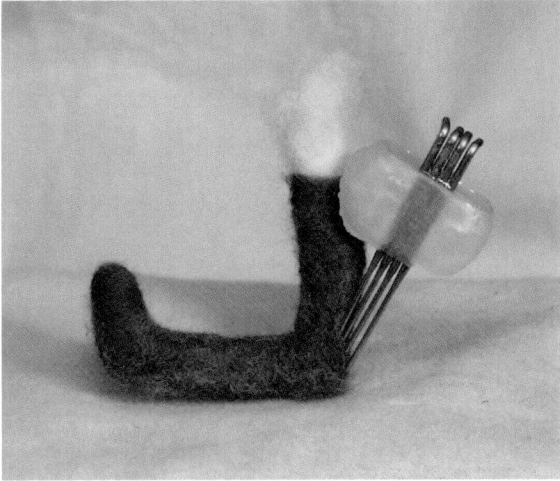

Creating an elbow or knee is done in the same manner as creating the foot. You begin needling where you want the turn to be, and then continue needling until the joint is well established.

Where you place these bends depends on the size of your beast, having reference photos available can help you make such decisions.

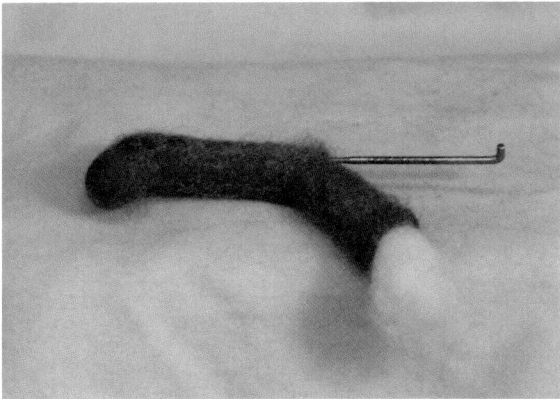

Even though eventually we will be adding more fiber which will help to felt this leg firmer, it is a good ideal to "stuff the tube" and do some very deep felting down the long center section.

The shoulder turn has been established on the leg.

See how much smaller in diameter the manipulated leg is in comparison to the un-worked leg.

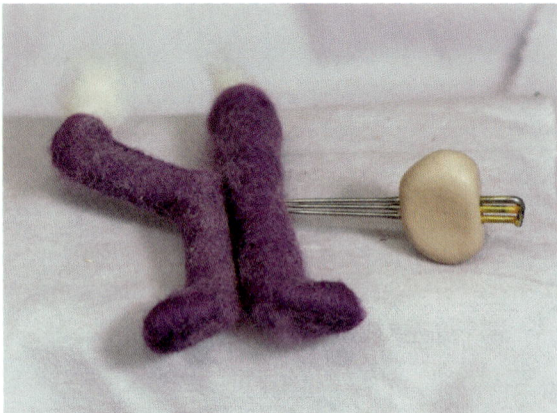

This completely felted leg can now become the guide for felting its partner.

By laying them back to back on your work surface you can easily see where you need to create the elbow turn on the second leg.

Pinning them in place to check proportions is always a wise step.

These legs look to be about the correct length but they are too thin for the dragon. Additional dress fiber will be added not only to correct the thinness but to also add additional strength.

Prior to adding more fiber it is very good idea to felt the legs even firmer! There is a bit of a problem with doing so: they are such an odd shape now that it would only be easy to felt them on the sides and the top of the shin, but you really want to uniformly felt from all sides.

What to do?

The solution is to create yourself some "rests".

"Rests" are firmly felted objects of whatever shape you need. Their purpose is to support the object being felted. Be careful not to felt into your rests.

Rests can also be created out of rigid foam if you really need to deep felt from an odd angle.

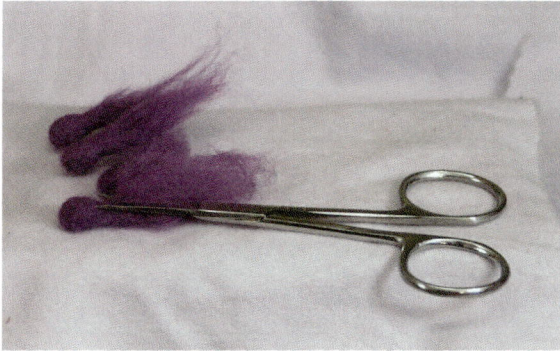

Toes: Using some carded fiber, needle to establish rounded end cylinders of the correct size and of medium firmness.

To add a bit more character, these toes were more firmly felted between what would be the second and third knuckles. The result is some nicely shaped toes but there is a lot of excess fiber on each of them.

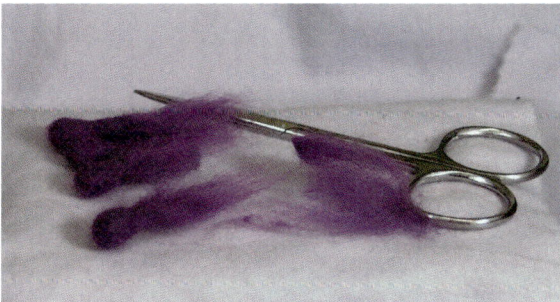

I have removed half of the fiber on the side that will lie against the foot.

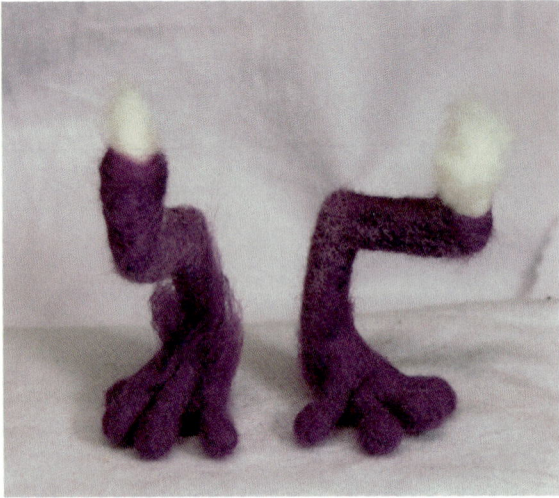

Laying the toes out on the work surface and lightly felting them together makes it easier to attach them to the foot, although if you prefer, you could attach each toe separately.

The leg on the right has the toes felted on while the leg on the left still displays the fiber from the toes that need to be felted into the foot and ankle.

These legs are getting pretty firm as is evident from the fact that they remain upright on their own. It still wouldn't hurt to felt for even more strength.

Now all four legs have been created and dressed with additional fiber.

Pinning the legs into place reveals what seemed to be the case many photos ago: the body isn't long enough for the dragon I had in mind.

It is easier to see what adjustments to the body are needed when you can pin the legs and head in place to check proportions.

Some additional fiber to the chest, rear end and neck are all in order.

What is a dragon without wings?
Chinese. (Chinese dragons fly without wings, I don't know how, but they do!)

This one however, needs wings, and to create them, a partial armature will be needed. The exposed portions of the armature are wrapped with fiber and felted. They will be re-wrapped for thickness and to create a neater finish.

Note the wire oval which will be used to attach the armature to the body.

All the parts are now pinned to the body as a last check for proportion. If changes are needed, now is the best time to make them.

Once satisfied it is time to start needling the parts into place. I like to do this with the parts pinned in place so they don't move until they are attached.

I always start with the legs and once I have them loosely attached, the pins are removed. Next I double check placement and make any corrections before deep needling them into the body.

Attaching the wings requires special attention. The wire oval which lies against the back was first covered with fiber and felted and then that itself was felted into the body.

A lot of fiber and felting will be done to secure the wing armatures into place and to make them disappear.

Note that I've left loose fiber at the top of the neck. Those fibers will be used to help attach the head to the neck.

Legs and wings are all deep felted into place and dressing fiber is added and felted as needed.

If you look closely, you can see a slight ridge on the back caused by the oval wire of the wing armature. This will completely disappear by adding more fiber.

Triangular scales were created using the flat felted triangle method and felted into place down the center of the back.

I really had hoped to do some additional sculpting on this dragon but the wings make that an extremely awkward task.

It could still be possible to use fiber to create skin patterns or scales.

I did create a couple of horns (which I wet felted for additional strength) but they just didn't seem to suit this little guy.

The more firmly felted your piece is, the more defined can be your sculpting be. Remember, that has to begin from a medium firm object which is gradually worked to very firm. Pinching the fibers with your fingers can also help when sculpting.

Rests:

Create your own rests as needed! Having a variety of rests available to support your project will allow you to felt from awkward angles without stressing your object. Rests can also be used under the brush mat to tilt the whole mat to a useful angle.

My own collection of rests is growing as I find need for new shapes and sizes. These are simple to make from core fiber and are firm to provide support without give.

Furring an object:

How about a mouse? The basic body shape is very simple and easily created with core fiber. This has been felted to medium firmness with the understanding that the additional felting needed to transform this into a mouse will make it smaller and firmer.

Furring is more easily done on a firm object!

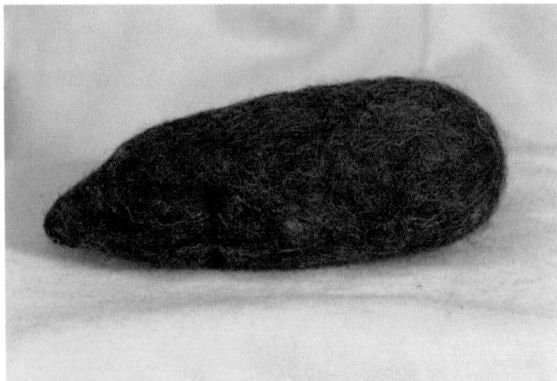

Some blended brown dressing fiber covers the whole. Two ears (free form flat felted) will help a lot to establish that this is a mouse. A tail and thin cylinders worked into legs are the only other major felted pieces that will be needed.

Black beads will make convincing eyes.

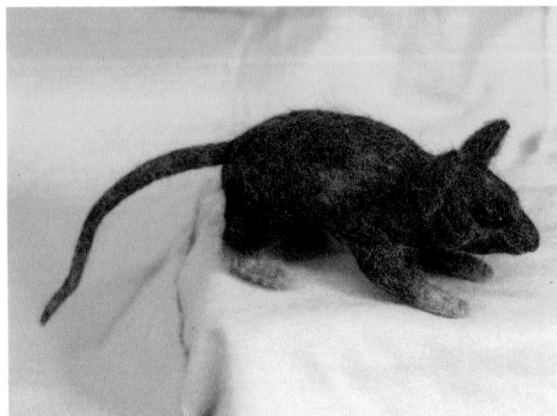

Here is the needle felted mouse – ready for fur.

I've tried felting with a number of fibers and have found that I like silk best. Wool fibers used for fur tend to want to felt down while silk (which can be felted) is more resistant.

I have not yet found a good source for dyed silk fiber in the colors I need so have learned to dye my own. Jacquard's Green Label Silk Dye is easy to use and requires no heat.

Fiber to be used for fur should be cut to a length at least twice as long as the finished fur. Lengths of 1" are excellent for most projects.

It must be long enough to hold the fiber ends between finger and thumbs and have enough of the tips free for felting.

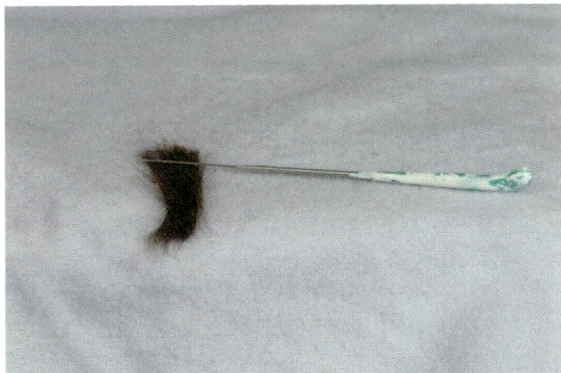

A #42 needle is used; it is fine enough to pick up just a few fibers at a time.

Here is another instance when it is imperative that you know where the first barb is on the needle. That barb should be the very first to pick up some of your furring fiber and enter into the object being furred.

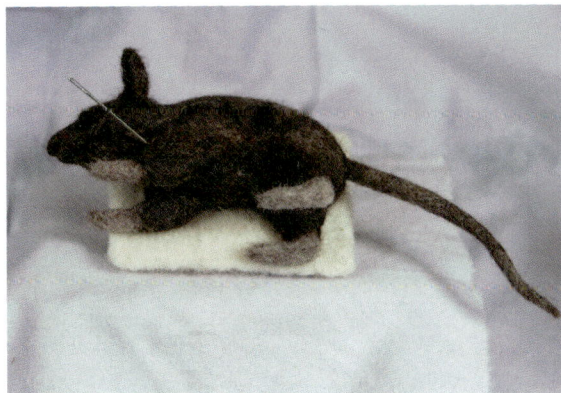

Furring creatures is awkward. It really is!

To assist in the process, I have numerous rests that are used to position the object to lessen the difficulties as much a possible.

Doll needles stuck right through the object and the rest help to hold everything in place. You will want the doll needle out of your way, yet positioned to resist the needling you will do to apply fur. Sometimes more than one doll needle is needed to secure your object in place.

Chapter Thirteen: Creating Fur

Think of how fur lies on the body. Generally fur grows to be streamlined.

Start furring at the tail and work towards the head.

Keeping the needle angle very shallow, insert the tip of the needle all the way in.

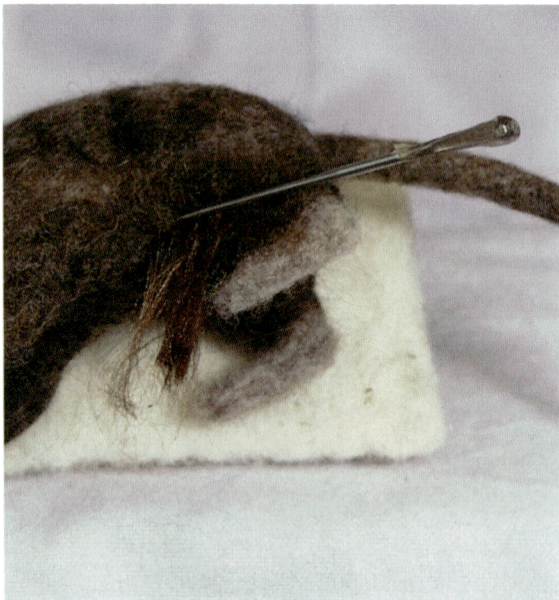

When you are working, the fiber ends away from the body would be held between your thumb and fingertips.

Lay the loose ends against the piece to be furred and catch just a few fibers in that first barb as you thrust the needle tip into the object.

Leave the tip of the needle in your object as you gently pull away the excess furring fiber.

Needle IN PLACE several times – don't completely remove the needle while you jab three of four times.

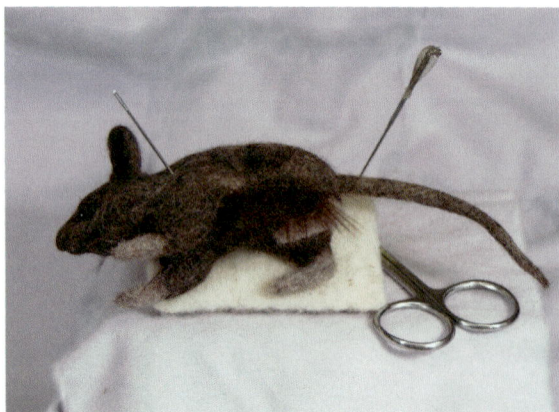

Do a few rows of fur. Some of the fiber will not have become secured and will fall out. This is normal.

I use my needle's barb to catch the loose _tips_ of the furring fibers. Others prefer to grab fibers perhaps a quarter inch from the tips or even in the middle of the furring fiber length.

Find what works most effectively for you.

Chapter Thirteen: Creating Fur

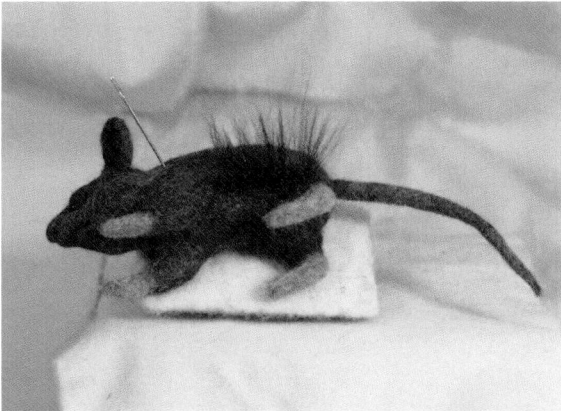

Gently fluff your rows of fur into the air – doing so will assist in trimming the fur to a uniform length.

I like to lift my brush mat, rest and object up so that I can clearly see where to trim.

You could just unpin your creature to do this but if you don't need to unpin and re-pin, you can resume furring more quickly.

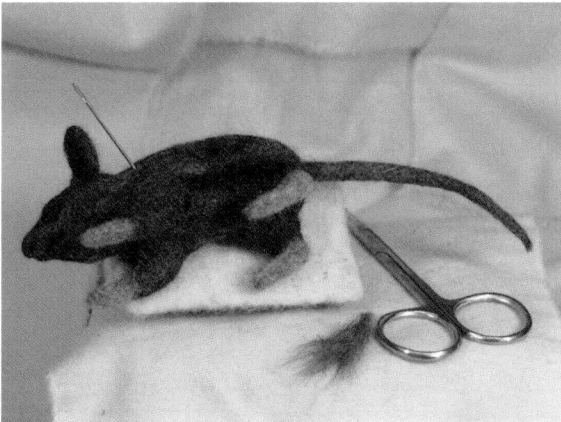

Now repeat the process of furring rows and trimming them to the desired length a zillion trillion times.

Do keep in mind the way real fur lies on a body. The orientation can actually change directions when you're furring legs. Instead of going from head (where the fur fiber is anchored into the body) to tail, on a leg it goes from shoulder (anchored) to toes.

When there is such a change in orientation, gradually change the direction in which you are rooting the fur as needed.

Sometimes you may wish to slightly alter the height of your trim. For this mouse I trimmed the fur shorter near the ankles and also around the face.

Fur that wants to stand up for whatever reason can be lightly surface felted down.

Chapter Thirteen: Creating Fur

I chose to do a mouse to demonstrate how to fur because a mouse is not an overly complicated shape and the legs are not long, making the whole thing fairly easy to fur. When you want to fur a creature that is far more complicated and going to have areas that will be nearly impossible to fur correctly, no matter how you try to position it on a rest, you have to take a completely different tactic.

To fur this Pritten it was necessary to fur the lower portions of the legs prior to attaching them to the body.

Likewise it was necessary to fur the stomach and neck areas before attaching the legs.

All of the tail was pre-furred except the base where it would be attached to the body.

Pre-furring such areas takes a bit of planning but certainly pays off.

Sassy

It is a good idea to just practice furring. Try different sized needles and different angles to learn what changes these variations cause to the appearance of the fur.

Try experimenting with different densities of fur to find what is best to provide the effect you desire.

Try trimming to different lengths.

Fur that is rooted into the object at a 90 degree angle tends to stand up more than fiber rooted at a shallow angle. Sometimes that can be useful.

Healing pieces:

This is a simple log or cylinder shape that was only surface felted.

Normally you would not and should not only surface felt an object. I've done so here to demonstrate not only the ease with which felted objects can be "healed" but to physically illustrate that those un-felted fibers are not adding strength to the object as a whole.

When it is cut open the fiber in the middle which was not felted expands and puffs out.

If you recall, I presented photos much earlier showing various ways of needling. I had cut those samples in half to reveal the needling. The core fiber in those samples did not expand at all because they had been properly deep felted.

The fiber can be forced back into place and the log/cylinder needled to close the cut.

You may notice that this log/cylinder is not as thick as in the earlier photo. Deep needling has caused a reduction in the diameter of the cylinder.

A small addition of fiber can be added to completely remove all traces of this log/cylinder ever having been cut open.

I could add more fiber if it was absolutely necessary that this cylinder be the same size it was originally.

Fiber is very forgiving as a medium. Don't be afraid to take something apart if it is wrong. I once completely removed and replaced a head on a furred figure because the original head was too small. If you didn't know that I had done this, you could not tell by looking at the finished figure.

Adding fiber is always easy! Removing excess fiber may seem more difficult but truly it is also easy. You can trim with sharp scissors or use a lint shaver to reduce the excess fiber.

Experiment:

I do understand that it is more rewarding to work on a project but sometimes it is worth the time, effort and materials to just experiment. Make samplers similar to the fur sampler pictured earlier and keep notes on what you have tried. Such samplers can be the most efficient means of learning and mastering techniques.

Finishing:

Flyaway fibers:

There always seem to be some flyaway fibers left on the surface no matter how diligently you felt.
Needling almost parallel to the surface with a #42 needle (remember where the first barb is located) can catch many of these fibers and felt them into the object. My Four Together tool does this job very well. You can just choose to leave the remaining flyaway fibers or you may choose to trim those fibers. A sweater saver works reasonably well for removing such fibers but cannot easily access all areas of a complex piece. Too much pressure on a sweater saver can also begin to remove fiber that you want to remain. Embroidery scissors work well and you just need to be patient as you attend to this task.

Solidity & Firmness:

Check your piece for solidity. Nothing should be at risk of falling off or coming apart from normal light handling. If your piece is meant to be a toy it should withstand rough handling without significant damage. If your piece has legs, they need to be solid enough to provide support.

The piece should be uniformly firm. There are reasonable exceptions. In the squash box that was created the stem is more firm than is the rest of the squash. This allowed for increased sculpting of the stem which provides both an attractive appearance and a good handle to the top. In the Pear Face the eyebrows are very loosely felted to provide a more realistic eyebrow appearance. No one is expected to be tearing them off so that works fine.

My Tools:

Throughout this book you have seen my multiple needle tools in many of the photographs. I have five needle tools that I use constantly. I actually have multiples that are set up with different sized needles so that I don't need to spend time swapping out needles.

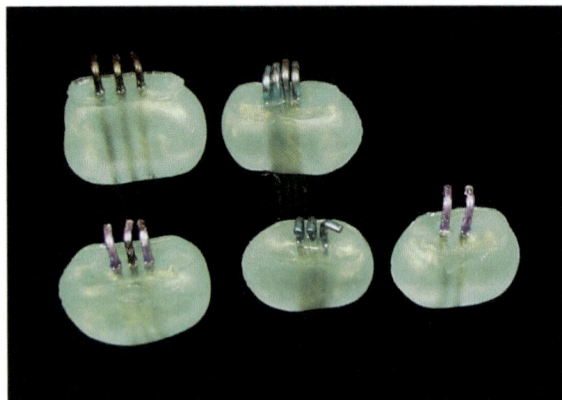

These tools are held between thumb and finger and are comfortable to hold for extended periods of time. They are easy to control and needle effectively.

There is sort of a Zen relationship between these tools and needle felting an object. At the beginning of a project the fiber occupies more physical space and contains a lot of open space. The best tool to use at this stage is the tool which also has more open space, i.e. the Three Wide Tool fitted with larger, coarser needles. As the fibers get felted together and open space is reduced, my tools that have less open space become more useful. As the project becomes increasingly felted the best tools are the Four Together or Three together tools fitted with finer needles.

Needles can be removed and replaced using needle nose pliers. Please exercise extreme care when adding or removing needles!

Three Wide Tool: This holds three needles parallel to one another spaced perhaps 1/8th of an inch apart. I use #38 star needles in this tool for initial deep felting. It is also my tool of choice for joining parts together. #36 needles would also work well in this tool

Three Medium Tool: This holds three needles parallel to one another, but spaced closer together than the previous tool. I have several of these tools fitted with different needles. These are excellent for felting thin cylinders.

Two Medium Tool: Similar to the tool above, this tool excels at making depressions and marking locations for Controlled Cutting. I have this tool fitted with #38 star needles.

Three Together Tool: On this tool three needles are placed side by side. At the tips there is still a bit of space in between each needle simply because the tips are narrower than the shanks. I have separate tools fitted with #38s, #40s and with #42s. This tool is excellent for fine sculpting when fitted with the finer needles. It is also very useful when a piece becomes too firmly felted to easily use the next tool.

Four Together Tool: Of all my tools, this one gets the most use. I always keep two of these tools close at hand, one loaded with #40 needles and the other with #42 needles. This is my tool of choice for surface felting and for finishing. It is also pretty good to use alternately with the Three Wide Tool during the initial felting process. It flat felts beautifully and quickly!

I hope to soon offer my tools for sale through CraftEdu.com and http://www.etsy.com/shop/IntimateForest

Walt Dizzy

Favorite Resources:

Mielke's Fiber Arts, LLC **Rudolph, WI 54475** http://www.mielkesfarm.com/index.htm	A great source for fibers and excellent prices!!
Frankenmuth Woolen Mill http://www.thewoolenmill.com/	Super source for core fiber! Sold as batting for quilts a crib size provides a lot of core fiber for a lot of projects! Sometimes contains some vegetable matter but still the best core fiber I have used!
Van Dykes Taxidermy **P.O. Box 367** **Woonsocket, SD 57385** http://www.vandykestaxidermy.com/	Great glass eyes in a wide variety of sizes!

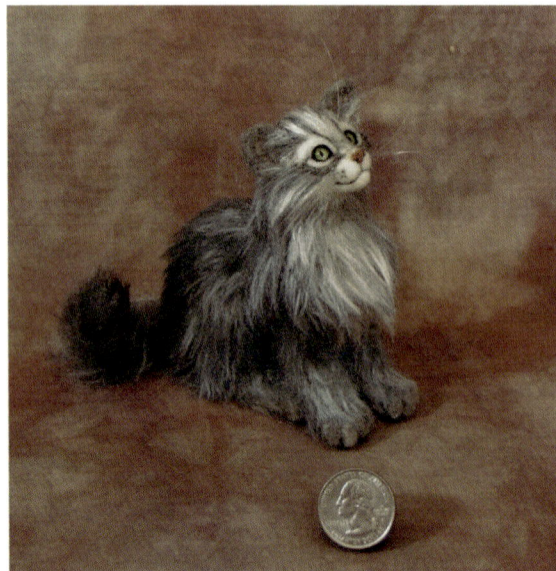

Gandalf

CPSIA information can be obtained
at www.ICGtesting.com
Printed in the USA
LVIC06n1933050115
421583LV00005B/75

9781451568172